Looking at Type®
Your Career

Charles R. Martin, Ph.D.

C A P T®

Center for Applications of Psychological Type, Inc.
Gainesville, Florida
www.capt.org

Published by
Center for Applications of Psychological Type, Inc.
2815 NW 13th Street, Suite 401
Gainesville, FL 32609-2815
352.375.0160

Center for Applications of Psychological Type, CAPT,
Looking at Type, and LAT are trademarks or registered
trademarks of the Center for Applications of Psychological
Type, Inc. in the United States and other countries.

Myers-Briggs Type Indicator, Myers-Briggs, and MBTI
are trademarks or registered trademarks of The Myers
& Briggs Foundation in the United States and other
countries.

Printed in the United States of America.

ISBN 13 978-0-935652-91-8

CONTENTS

FOREWORD

This book is intended for those who want to use psychological type to explore career options—to find, develop, and/or manage their career. A variety of people will find it helpful: students considering a first-time job, young adults who are already working and who want to find out more about career options, and adults who have been working in careers for several years but who are considering changes in roles or careers.

People invest an enormous amount of time and energy in their work. Thus, the ideal situation is to be involved in a career and in roles that are rewarding, enjoyable, and make use of one's natural talents. Type can help you find just such a career and identify those kinds of roles.

A quick review of the Myers-Briggs Type Indicator® (MBTI®) instrument and type theory is provided in this book, but if you want additional information, *Looking at Type®: The Fundamentals* provides the kind of introduction to these topics that you need.

In the pages that follow, type will be used to help you understand yourself and your natural preferences and to understand how those preferences relate to your career exploration, decision making, development, and management.

You will also see that type differences are all valuable and that no combination of type preferences is better than any other combination of preferences. Each of the sixteen types has its own strengths and potential blind spots, and in this book you will see how you can make use of your strengths and work through your blind spots. Many people find that upon discovering their true type, there is a feeling of "fit" and a sense of relief as they understand that their likes and dislikes, ways of interacting, and goals and behaviors are all natural extensions of their combination of preferences. Type can also help you find this sense of "fit" in your career. You may find this fit through using type to help choose a career niche, or through learning how to modify how you work so that the needs generated by your type preferences are better met.

As you read this book, remember that *you* are the expert on who you are and what your type preferences are. You are also the one who will ultimately decide how you express your type in whatever career you choose. We wish you the best in your career exploration and career management.

ACKNOWLEDGEMENTS

for her ongoing support and presence in my life, and for her wisdom and insight into people, I want to express gratitude to my wife and life partner, Tamara. Our amazing daughter—for whom I am forever grateful—is an ongoing reminder of the joys of following your path and doing what you love.

I would also like to express appreciation to the wide range of people who contributed knowledge, editorial review, and support during the development and completion of this project. Thanks go to Tom Thompson for his editing and input into the first edition of this book, and to Ron Walsh and colleagues and Jamelyn Johnson for their reviews of the manuscript and their helpful comments. The publication of this book could not have happened without funding in part by a grant from the Human Resource Research Institute in Tokyo, Japan. Thanks also go to Eleanor Sommer for her editing of the second edition of this work.

Special thanks go to Mary McCaulley and Jerry Macdaid, whose extensive knowledge and experience with type, and whose willingness to share those, helped make this book possible. Their presence, support and belief in me has helped me to create a career that is an extension of who I am.

Acknowledgement also goes to the intellectual legacy and person of Isabel Myers, whose ground-breaking work formed the basis for the applications of type described in this book. Finally, acknowledgement and appreciation go to the countless friends, colleagues, and clients who have contributed both directly and indirectly to the development of this book.

INTRODUCTION

One of Isabel Myers' earliest goals for the MBTI® instrument was to help people choose careers that would be interesting to them and would call on their strengths. Ongoing research with individuals and the MBTI instrument has confirmed that there are very real type differences in how people learn and how they work. Research shows there are patterns in the different types of how they choose or avoid various occupations. You will be introduced to these patterns later in this book.

Research *also* shows that every personality type can be found in any given career, and so it's particularly important to recognize that there are type differences in the *kinds* of tasks, roles, and environments that people enjoy—regardless of career area. Perhaps most important, there are type differences in the way people approach all of the activities needed to develop and manage their careers. Grasping these differences empowers you to make informed decisions about your career development. You can determine if the choices you are making are supporting you or are getting in the way of an ultimately satisfying career path.

The bottom line for the application of psychological type in your career exploration is expressed in two phrases often used by Isabel Myers: "gifts differing," and "the constructive use of differences." A career is one place where we can find expression for our differing gifts—our unique personal qualities and talents. In addition, since a career provides us with opportunities to work with people whose qualities and talents differ from our own, an understanding of type can help us to blend and make use of those differences in constructive ways.

The different sections of this book address some major steps in your career development and management. Essentially, you need to learn about who you are, gather information on your career options, make decisions about where you want to go, and follow through on the decisions you make by having goals and taking concrete action. This book is designed to help you understand and make use of type at every one of these steps.

As you read this book, you will want to respect your own natural tendencies, and explore your career options in a way that makes use of the strengths of your type. In addition, you will also want to have a healthy respect for the potential blind spots that can be associated with your particular type preferences.

And finally, since we believe in the value and power of the different personality types, we encourage you to approach this book in a way that fits for you and your own type preferences. That is, go to the parts that most appeal to you, and approach those sections in an order that makes sense to you. In addition, since our type preferences cause us to prefer some kinds of information over others, please be aware that the activities in this book that you most want to skip may be *particularly helpful* to someone with your type preferences!

Looking at Yourself

1ooking at yourself means gaining understanding of who you are through exploring key dimensions that are important in successful career development and career management. The five dimensions you will explore in this book are (1) personality type, (2) values, (3) interests, (4) skills, and (5) type dynamics and development.

The MBTI® Instrument and the Basic Language of Type

In this section you will learn more about the MBTI® instrument and the four preferences that are the basis for your personality type.

Each question on the MBTI assessment provides equally valuable choices and asks you to indicate which appeals to you more. The questions let you indicate a preference on four dichotomous (either/or) scales: Extraversion or Introversion, Sensing or Intuition, Thinking or Feeling, and Judging or Perceiving. There are no right or wrong answers; they simply represent preferences. When the MBTI instrument is scored, the combination of preferences on the four scales indicates one of sixteen types.

The best way to assess your type preferences is to take the MBTI assessment and to have a professional verify the results of your four letter type through a personal conversation with you. (See the list of resources at the end of this book.) It is also not uncommon for people to have taken the MBTI instrument and to have forgotten their results. Not to worry, in the upcoming section, the four basic preference pairs and the theory of psychological type will be explained.

On each scale, there are two different choices, or preferences. Everyone uses both choices at one time or another, but each person naturally prefers one of the choices over the other, just as people are naturally right-handed or left-handed.

As you read the following descriptions of the four pairs of preferences, see if you can recognize which of each pair is your most natural preference. You will be given the opportunity to make a note of each of your preferences to help prompt your responses as you work through the rest of the book.

Extraversion (E)   Introversion (I)

Following are examples of qualities and behaviors often associated with Extraversion and Introversion. Check any that apply to you.

EXTRAVERSION People with a preference for Extraversion . . .

❑ Direct energy mostly to the people and things in the "outside world."

❑ Like involvement in many activities. May find that the draw of other activities can disturb their concentration.

❑ Are often drawn to work in positions with high people contact, out-of-office activities, and variety.

❑ Are attracted to careers where action and interaction are important, such as business, sales, marketing, service fields, public relations, politics, and government.

❑ May be drawn to discuss their career options and plans with others because it helps clarify what they want and where they are going.

EXTRAVERSION (E) _____

INTROVERSION People with a preference for Introversion . . .

❑ Direct energy mostly to the ideas in their minds.

❑ May find that they can concentrate for long periods of time. They may like focusing on one activity in depth and dislike interruptions.

❑ Are often drawn to work requiring solo activities or one-to-one contact, continuity, and concentration.

❑ Are attracted to careers where ideas are important, such as college teaching, information technology, writing, research, science, and engineering.

❑ May be drawn to a great deal of quiet, careful, and private reflection on their career options as a way of clarifying what they want and where they are going.

INTROVERSION (I) _____

Given that we all *sometimes* extravert and *sometimes* introvert, do your answers to these questions indicate that a natural preference for Extraversion or Introversion fits you better?

Direction of Energy:
Extraversion (E) or Introversion (I)

Extraversion comes from the Latin for "outward turning." When we are extraverting, our energy goes out to the world around us. The outer world draws our attention and interest. We notice what is happening, and like to jump into action.

Introversion comes from the Latin for "inward turning." When we are introverting, our energy goes inward toward the concepts and ideas that help explain the world around us. The inner world draws our attention and interest. We want a clear idea of what is happening before we move into action.

Sensing (S)	Intuition (N)

Following are examples of qualities and behaviors that often come from preferring and developing either Sensing perception or Intuitive perception. Check any that apply to you.

SENSING PERCEPTION People with a preference for Sensing . . .

❑ Are often seen as realistic and practical, and good at grasping the facts and details.

❑ Focus more on the present than the future.

❑ Are often patient and careful with precise work and routines, and they like the chance to hone a skill.

❑ Tend to seek education that has practical uses. They are more likely to prefer hands-on training.

❑ Are attracted to careers where they can be involved in production, management of a business or service, construction, office administration and accounting, patient care, police work, and other areas where hands-on activities are needed to solve immediate problems.

❑ Are often attentive to the facts of a job, or role, in their career development and often focus on what is a good fit for now, or on what is available in the very near future.

SENSING (S) _____

INTUITIVE PERCEPTION People with a preference for Intuition . . .

❑ Are often seen as imaginative and insightful, and good at grasping the big picture.

❑ Focus more on the future than on the present.

❑ Are often patient in projects with many intangibles and possibilities, and they enjoy new ways of doing things.

❑ Tend to enjoy knowledge for its own sake. They are more likely to pursue higher education.

❑ Are attracted to careers where theory or recognition of patterns are important, as in counseling, journalism, teaching, writing, art, religion, science, research, law, or areas where long-range planning in business or policy development are required.

❑ Are often attentive to the potential of a job or role in their career development, and often focus on long-term career possibilities and options.

INTUITION (N) _____

Given that we use both Sensing and Intuition everyday, does a natural preference for Sensing or Intuition fit you better?

The Tools of Perception:
Sensing (S) and Intuition (N)

In type theory, there are two primary ways of taking in information: Sensing and Intuition. People tend to trust one of these kinds of information over the other. Your preference for Sensing perception or Intuitive perception can have an effect on which careers you tend to enjoy.

Sensing is the tool of the mind that deals with the present reality. Sensing refers to the information we take in with our senses—what we see, hear, smell, touch, and taste, as well as the kinesthetic sense of our bodies. Individuals with a preference for Sensing often develop excellent powers of observation, and may also develop gifts of reality, practicality, common sense, and working in the here-and-now. Intuition is the opposite kind of perception from Sensing. Intuition is the tool of the mind that lets us see beyond the present and imagine what has never been before. It lets us deal with symbols and abstractions. Individuals with a preference for Intuition often develop skills of imagination, and may also develop gifts in working with symbols, meanings, patterns, and in seeing possibilities.

Thinking (T)	Feeling (F)

Following are examples of qualities and behaviors that often come from preferring and developing either Thinking judgment or Feeling judgment. Check any that apply to you.

THINKING JUDGMENT People with a preference for Thinking . . .	FEELING JUDGMENT People with a preference for Feeling . . .
❏ Prefer to understand experience through logical thinking.	❏ Prefer to understand experience in the context of human relationships.
❏ Seek truth and fairness, regardless of effect, and may be seen as forthright and firm.	❏ Seek harmony and cooperation, sometimes ignoring the consequences; may be seen as warm and understanding.
❏ Naturally critique to detect errors or inconsistencies.	❏ Naturally appreciate the merits of others.
❏ Are often drawn to education in fields where logical analysis and a fair-minded approach to ideas, things, numbers, or persons are the focus. Also found in all fields of education.	❏ Are often drawn to education in fields where communication and a more personal approach to, and involvement with, people are the focus. However, they are found in all fields of education.
❏ Are often attracted to careers in trades and crafts, science and technology, computers, production, management, law, protective services, and criminal justice work.	❏ Are often attracted to careers in teaching, health care, office and administrative work, personal and human services, communication, entertainment, counseling, and the ministry.
❏ Want to make career development decisions using logic and a fair-minded consideration of the alternatives to reach the right conclusions.	❏ Want to make career development decisions based on what is most important in their lives and the consequences for them personally and for the people they care about.

THINKING (T) _____   **FEELING** (F) _____

Given that we all use both Thinking and Feeling at times, does a natural preference for Thinking judgment or Feeling judgment fit you better?

The Tools of Judgment: Thinking (T) and Feeling (F)

When we have established from our Sensing perception what is, and from our Intuitive perception what might be, it is time to use our judgment to make decisions for action. There are two tools for making decisions—Thinking and Feeling.

Thinking judgment is an impersonal approach for making decisions. Problems are examined from an outside point of view—looking at consequences in a fair-minded way. Thinking uses logical analysis to determine likely cause-and-effect outcomes of the possible options. It puts choices in a rational order on the basis of more to less accurate, often with the goal of finding out what is impartially "true."

Feeling judgment is a more personal approach for making decisions. Feeling is concerned with what matters—the long-term good and the short-term good. Feeling reaches decisions by weighing the value of various options—what is worthwhile—and often by putting in the forefront what the people involved care about. Feeling puts choices in a rational order, based on a continuum of more to less valuable, often with the goal of determining what is "important." In MBTI theory, we need to remember that Feeling is a rational mental process for making decisions and does not mean *emotion*.

Judging (J)	Perceiving (P)

Following are examples of qualities and behaviors that are often associated with a preference for either Judging or Perceiving. Check any that apply to you.

THE JUDGING LIFESTYLE People with a preference for Judging . . .	THE PERCEIVING LIFESTYLE People with a preference for Perceiving . . .
❑ Value order, structure, and predictability, and like the completion of tasks.	❑ Value spontaneity and the challenge of dealing with the unexpected, and don't want to rush to closure.
❑ Want matters decided and settled, and take deadlines and schedules seriously.	❑ Like to leave options open and may let other interesting developments interfere with deadlines.
❑ Tolerate, and may even enjoy, routine.	❑ Find routine boring, even intolerable.
❑ Are often found in management jobs—but may be found in any field.	❑ Are often found in troubleshooting jobs—but may be found in any field.
❑ Are attracted to work settings where plans, system, order, and deadlines are important, and they are often drawn to tasks where they can assume responsibility.	❑ Are attracted to work settings where change, flexibility, and innovation are important, and they are often drawn to tasks where they can work independently.
❑ Approach their career development in a planful way, through setting and pursuing identifiable career tasks and goals.	❑ Approach career development in a flexible way, through exploring their options and responding adaptively to what emerges on their career path.
JUDGING (J) _____	**PERCEIVING (P)** _____

Given that our lifestyles reflect both Judging and Perceiving at times, does a natural preference for a Judging lifestyle or a Perceiving lifestyle fit you better?

Two Orientations to the World: Judging (J) and Perceiving (P)

There are two different lifestyle orientations to the outer world—Judging and Perceiving. Everyone goes back and forth between the Perceiving mode and the Judging mode, but Perceiving types stay longer in the information-gathering mode, while Judging types move more quickly to the decision-making mode. As a result, Perceiving types often look more flexible, open, and adaptable, while Judging types often look more structured, organized, and closure seeking. In type language, Judging means "preferring to make decisions," and not "judgmental," as in the common use of the word. In like fashion, Perceiving means "preferring to gather information," and not "perceptive," as in the common use of the word.

Clarifying Your Preferences

Often people are not clear about what they like, but are clearer about what they don't like or what is stressful for them. If you are having difficulty figuring out your type preferences, you can ask yourself the following kinds of questions:

1) If I had to choose, would it be more difficult for me to (a) work with a group of people all day (if so, you might be an I), or (b) work alone all day (if so, you might be an E)?

2) Would it be more stressful for me to (a) pay attention to the facts and realities all of the time (if so, you might be an N), or (b) come up with new ideas and approaches all of the time (if so, you might be an S)?

3) Is it more difficult for me to (a) constantly step outside the situation and analyze it impersonally (if so, you might be an F), or (b) be continually concerned with the impact of events on individuals in my life (if so, you might be a T)?

4) If I had to choose, would it be more stressful for me to (a) adhere to a schedule during the day, even one I created (if so, you might be a P), or (b) continually have to adapt to changing work conditions (if so, you might be a J)?

Make a note in the following space about what your four type preferences are or might be.

My preferences are:

E or I _____   **S or N** _____   **T or F** _____   **J or P** _____

Write a brief statement about what your preferences may mean for your career choice. You might want to discuss this with someone who also knows type.

_____

_____

_____

_____

_____

For matching yourself to a career, position, or role that will draw out the best in you, you need to *know more about yourself* than your type preferences. Understanding your values, interests, and skills—in conjunction with knowledge of your type—will provide you with the beginning information you need to make good career decisions. This applies to career *choice*, as well as to career *development and management*.

This is why the next section encourages you to make an assessment of your values, interests, and skills. Then you can integrate that information with knowledge of your type.

Even more than using it to match you to a career or role, type can be especially powerful when you use it to understand *how* you might approach *all* the steps you need to take to find, develop, and manage your career. You can use knowledge of your type to help you understand how to approach gathering information, exploring options, networking, decision making, goal setting, and taking action.

Values, Interests, and Skills

As previously mentioned, your MBTI type provides you with the first basic dimension for looking at yourself. Your personality type, however, is only one part of the larger process of self-understanding. In the exploration of careers, individuals also need to be concerned with some other dimensions, for instance, their values, interests, skills, as well as the dynamics of their type.

Your Values

Values are those enduring characteristics or aspects of life and work that we consider important, even essential, to our satisfaction. What motivates you and would make a career worthwhile? In other words, what makes you get up in the morning? What do you *really* care about?

There are often relationships between a person's type preferences and the kinds of values that person holds. However, it should be understood that knowledge of your values should also *add* to information gained from knowledge of your psychological type. Thus, if you are an ESTJ, you may be inclined to share some values with other ESTJs, but you will also differ in values from other ESTJs. Psychological type is not a pigeon hole, and two ESTJs can *differ widely* in career paths based on differences in their values.

Take a look at the values checklist (on the next page) and reflect for a moment on what things are important for you as you think about a career. What do you value? What motivates you? Knowledge of your values helps refine your understanding of who you are and what you want.

For example, an ENFJ whose highest values are creativity, recognition, and self-expression might consider an acting career. In this fashion, the ENFJ's values are met, and they can utilize their natural preferences. On the other hand, an ENFJ whose highest values are family, spirituality, and nurturing others might be more satisfied in a career in the clergy rather than in acting, or some other setting where they can attend to the spiritual and emotional needs of others.

On the following page, write your highest ranked values in the spaces provided. How does this information add to or clarify your understanding of yourself, potential work settings, and careers you may be considering? How might you pursue them? You may also want to discuss these with someone else.

Values Checklist

On the following list, check your top ten to fifteen values. Of those, consider which ones you *really must have* in your life and career? Circle the top five.

- ❏ Achievement
- ❏ Adventure–Daring
- ❏ Aesthetics–Beauty
- ❏ Affiliation–Connection
- ❏ Authenticity
- ❏ Autonomy–Independence
- ❏ Broadmindedness
- ❏ Challenge
- ❏ Comfort
- ❏ Cooperation
- ❏ Competition
- ❏ Contribution to society
- ❏ Creativity
- ❏ Curiosity
- ❏ Devotion
- ❏ Enjoyment
- ❏ Environment–Nature
- ❏ Equality
- ❏ Ethics
- ❏ Excitement–Stimulation

- ❏ Expertise–Competence
- ❏ Fairness
- ❏ Fame
- ❏ Family
- ❏ Forgiveness
- ❏ Freedom
- ❏ Friendship
- ❏ Generosity
- ❏ Health
- ❏ Helping others
- ❏ Honesty
- ❏ Honor
- ❏ Humility
- ❏ Influence
- ❏ Inner harmony
- ❏ Integrity–Ethics
- ❏ Intelligence
- ❏ Leadership
- ❏ Leisure time
- ❏ Love–Compassion

- ❏ Loyalty
- ❏ Meaning in life
- ❏ Moderation
- ❏ Nurturing others
- ❏ Order–Structure
- ❏ Patriotism
- ❏ Peace
- ❏ Personal development
- ❏ Physical fitness
- ❏ Play
- ❏ Pleasure
- ❏ Politeness
- ❏ Power–Authority
- ❏ Prestige–Status
- ❏ Privacy
- ❏ Public contact
- ❏ Reciprocation of favors
- ❏ Recognition
- ❏ Respect of others
- ❏ Respect for tradition

- ❏ Responsibility
- ❏ Security
- ❏ Self-actualization
- ❏ Self-discipline
- ❏ Self-expression
- ❏ Self-respect
- ❏ Sense of belonging
- ❏ Service
- ❏ Social justice
- ❏ Social order–Structure
- ❏ Spirituality
- ❏ Stability
- ❏ Status
- ❏ Success
- ❏ Variety
- ❏ Wealth

  Other values not listed
- ❏ _____
- ❏ _____
- ❏ _____

YOUR VALUES. *Write your highest ranked values in the following spaces. How does this information add to or clarify your understanding of yourself, potential work settings, and careers you may be considering? How might you pursue them? You may also want to discuss these with someone else.*

_____

_____

_____

_____

_____

_____

_____

_____

_____

_____

_____

_____

Work Environment Preferences

A career or job can differ in look and feel depending on the environment in which you work. The work environment you prefer includes the organizational culture, interpersonal climate and the style and values of the people around you. Your satisfaction and success in a career are linked to your sense of fit with your environment.

To begin getting a sense of what your preferences are in this domain, have a look at the work environment checklist and then on the following page write your highest ranked environment preferences. Knowing your work environment preferences can give you ideas about what you want to move *toward* in your career and/or how you might make changes in your current environment (e.g., shift roles and responsibilities, take on different tasks, or changing jobs).

How does this information add to or clarify your understanding of yourself, potential work settings, and careers you may be considering? How will you find or create an environment that has the qualities most important to you? You may also want to discuss these with someone else.

Work Environment Preferences Checklist

On the following list, check your top ten to fifteen work environment preferences—what do you want around you in your work environment? Of those, consider which ones you feel you *really must have*— which ones can't you do without? Circle the top five.

❑ Achievement	❑ Fairness	❑ Making decisions	❑ Status
❑ Accuracy	❑ Fame	❑ Nurturing–Helping others	❑ Success
❑ Adventure–Excitement	❑ Fast pace	❑ Physically challenging–Demanding	❑ Structured–Orderly environment
❑ Advancement	❑ Financial security	❑ Physically comfortable	❑ Supportive environment
❑ Affiliation–Connection	❑ Flexible environment	❑ Playful	❑ Supports desired lifestyle
❑ Aesthetically appealing–Attractive environment	❑ Forgiveness	❑ Polite	❑ Time spent at work
❑ Authenticity	❑ Freedom	❑ Power–Authority	❑ Time–Freedom
❑ Autonomy–Independence	❑ Friendship	❑ Prestige–Recognition	❑ Tolerance–Broadmindedness
❑ Challenging problems	❑ Fun	❑ Producing something	❑ Tradition is valued
❑ Change and variety	❑ Generosity	❑ Privacy	❑ Tranquil environment
❑ Closeness to power	❑ Helping others	❑ Public contact	❑ Variety
❑ Community–Cooperation	❑ High earnings–Wealth opportunities	❑ Recognition	❑ Working alone
❑ Competition	❑ Influence others	❑ Respect from others	❑ Working with others
❑ Contribution to society	❑ Integrity–Ethics	❑ Respect for tradition	❑ Working on the frontiers of knowledge
❑ Control	❑ Intellectual pursuits	❑ Responsibility	❑ Working under pressure
❑ Creative expression	❑ Own interests–Skills are used	❑ Security	❑ Other environmental preferences not listed
❑ Exercising competence–Expertise	❑ Leadership	❑ Self-actualization	❑ _____
❑ Entrepreneurial activity	❑ Learning opportunities	❑ Self-expression	❑ _____
❑ Ethics	❑ Leisure time	❑ Sense of belonging	❑ _____
❑ Excitement	❑ Location–Geography	❑ Service (social or other)	
❑ Exhibition	❑ Loyalty	❑ Spiritual–Religious beliefs	
		❑ Stability	

YOUR WORK ENVIRONMENT PREFERENCES. *Write your highest ranked work environment preferences in the following spaces. How might you pursue them? You may also want to discuss these with someone else.*

_____

_____

_____

_____

_____

_____

_____

_____

_____

_____

_____

_____

_____

_____

_____

_____

_____

_____

_____

_____

_____

_____

_____

_____

_____

Your Interests

Your interests are those areas of work and/or study that naturally attract you. Interests include the kinds of tasks you like, the areas of thought that engage you, and the occupational areas that excite you. Grasping your career interests (that is, your passions and enthusiasms) is an important key to career satisfaction: the areas and activities that you *like* are what motivate you in the long run.

Take a look at the interest area checklist, and make an informal assessment of your interests. Or you may have already taken an interest inventory and you can use that information. As we noted in the discussion of

Interest Area Checklist

Which two or three of the following six areas best describe how you see yourself? Rank the top two or three areas.

☐ **Realistic (R)—Building and Doing**

People who have mechanical and athletic interests and abilities. Prefer to work with objects, machines, or tools rather than people or ideas. Prefer working with plants or animals, or being outdoors. More oriented to the present than to the future.

Typical careers: military, law enforcement, farming, forestry, agriculture, veterinary medicine, athletics, emergency response, trades and crafts, mechanics, transportation, architecture, and engineering.

☐ **Investigative (I)—Analyzing and Examining**

People who like to observe, analyze, and learn. Enjoy investigating, evaluating, and understanding. May have scholarly or academic interests. Prefer original approaches to problem solving and may have a high level of verbal and scientific skill.

Typical careers: computer science, medical technology, physical and life sciences, teaching science, medicine and allied health professions, dentistry, nursing, veterinary medicine, research, mathematics, college professor, psychology, and social sciences.

☐ **Artistic (A)—Creating and Symbolizing**

People who are artistic, innovative, expressive, and imaginative. Like to use their intuitive abilities and like to work in unstructured situations using their creativity. May be nonconforming and have artistic or musical skills.

Typical careers: fine and commercial artist, art teacher, illustrator, interior design, photography, music, chef, writer/journalist, drama and entertainment, English and foreign languages teacher, marketing/advertising, public relations, beautician, architecture, law.

☐ **Social (S)—Helping and Supporting**

People who are interested in and like to work with people. Like teaching, informing, enlightening, helping people develop, and curing others. Are often sensitive to the needs of others and are usually verbally and socially skilled.

Typical careers: counseling, social work, ministry, foreign language teaching, elementary teacher, nursing, dental hygiene, special education, social science teaching, physical education, school administration, occupational therapy, speech pathology.

☐ **Enterprising (E)—Persuading, Entrepreneurship, and Influencing**

People who like influencing, persuading, or leading others. Often possess verbal skills and act confidently in social situations. May highly value political or economic goals and enjoy taking action toward—or managing for—organizational goals or economic gain.

Typical careers: politics and public office, law, insurance agent, personnel and human resources, sales, purchasing, business management, restaurant management, chef, beautician, florist, real estate, marketing, nursing facility administration, agricultural management.

☐ **Conventional (C)—Structuring and Organizing**

People who tend to be precise and organized. Like structure and may tend to value material possessions and economic achievement. Enjoy working with data, and often have organizing or numerical abilities. Are good at carrying out details and bringing concrete tasks to conclusion.

Typical careers: banking, accounting, business education, nursing facility administration, food service management, credit management, office administration and support, military, dental assisting, mathematics, teaching, dietician.

values, remember that all ESTJs are not alike. While ESTJs all share some things in common, individual ESTJs can have quite different career paths depending on the differences in their career interests. Thus, whether the MBTI instrument and interest assessments *appear* to agree or not, a fuller picture of who you are is the result.

Individual career interests, and work environments as well, can be grouped into some combination of six broad areas. These categories are widely used in career inventories and in collections of career information; knowing your interest areas can point you in helpful directions in your career exploration. The six areas are Realistic, Investigative, Artistic, Social, Enterprising, and Conventional. At this point, stop and look through the list of career interest areas on the previous page. What are your top areas?

Since the categories in this interest area checklist were developed specifically with careers in mind, you will want to give a great deal of weight to this kind of information in making decisions about your career development, jobs, and roles.

Here again, knowledge of your interests helps broaden your sense of who you are. For example, a person with ISTJ type preferences may have interests in the physical sciences, research, and teaching. Though teaching might not be predicted on the basis of type alone, this new information must be considered in looking at possible careers. This ISTJ might consider teaching physics or chemistry in a university. Another ISTJ who has interests in business, mathematics, and finance might rather consider a career in accounting. Though these are overly simple examples, we see that each person is considering a career field where they could also make good use of their type preferences.

If your type preferences and interest areas don't seem to "match" each other, you may want to ask yourself some of the following kinds of questions.

What might be the source of the inconsistency? Have my family, friends, life experiences, and environment influenced my interests? Is that influence one that supports me or takes me away from my natural interests?

How might my interests and type preferences be usefully integrated? For example, could I find a way of working in a career interest area that would allow me to make use of my type preferences? Could I find a niche within that career field that allows me to express my type?

In the following page, write your top interest areas and a brief statement about how each of these areas interests you. Also note how you might find or create a career or role that makes use of those interests. What do these areas mean for your career exploration, development and management? You may find it helpful to discuss these areas with someone else.

YOUR INTEREST AREAS. *Write your highest interest areas in the following spaces. How does this information add to or clarify your understanding of yourself, potential work settings, and careers you may be considering? How might you pursue them? You may also want to discuss these with someone else.*

Read through the following lists of talents and skills. Which skills do you actually have (check those) and which do you want to keep doing or do more of in your career or job (circle those)? People have skills across all domains, so don't be concerned with whether the skills match your interest areas.

❏ Realistic (R)—Skills in the Building and Doing area

- ❏ Crafting/creating with materials
- ❏ Constructing/modeling rooms
- ❏ Eye-hand coordination
- ❏ Strength/stamina
- ❏ Whole body agility/coordination
- ❏ Operating/driving machinery
- ❏ Physical risk/daring
- ❏ Athletic ability
- ❏ Skills with tools
- ❏ Mechanical knowledge and skills
- ❏ Skills with plants and animals

❏ Investigative (I)—Skills in the Analyzing and Examining area

- ❏ Researching/investigating
- ❏ Analyzing information/data
- ❏ Generating/creating ideas
- ❏ Breaking data down into parts
- ❏ Forming data parts into wholes
- ❏ Finding patterns in data
- ❏ Building theoretical models
- ❏ Verbal skills
- ❏ Problem solving skills
- ❏ Consulting/advising in area of expertise

❏ Artistic (A)—Skills in the Creating and Symbolizing area

- ❏ Writing
- ❏ Entertaining
- ❏ Visualizing and spatial skills
- ❏ Acting/performing/singing
- ❏ Musical skills
- ❏ Imagining
- ❏ Innovating
- ❏ Designing
- ❏ Verbal skills
- ❏ Expressing ideas in words, pictures, stories

❏ Social (S)—Skills in the Helping and Supporting area

- ❏ Teaching/training
- ❏ Translating/interpreting others' ideas
- ❏ Informing/advising
- ❏ Assessing/evaluating others
- ❏ Motivating/inspiring
- ❏ Helping/supporting others
- ❏ Counseling/coaching
- ❏ Developing/mentoring others
- ❏ Providing service
- ❏ Healing/curing others
- ❏ Listening to and understanding others
- ❏ Demonstrating empathy
- ❏ Conversing/connecting easily
- ❏ Verbal skills
- ❏ Building harmonious relationships
- ❏ Facilitating interactions between others

❏ Enterprising (E)—Skills in the Persuading, Entrepreneurship, and Influencing area

- ❏ Influencing/persuading others
- ❏ Leading in teams or organizations
- ❏ Taking the lead socially
- ❏ Feeling comfortable with personal/financial risk
- ❏ Public speaking
- ❏ Supervising/managing
- ❏ Initiating/starting things
- ❏ Negotiating/debating
- ❏ Demonstrating political astuteness
- ❏ Producing/getting things done

❏ Conventional (C)—Skills in the Structuring and Organizing area

- ❏ Gathering/searching for and retrieving data
- ❏ Organizing/systematizing information
- ❏ Computing numbers/calculating
- ❏ Organizing spaces/environments
- ❏ Prioritizing/planning
- ❏ Noticing/remembering details
- ❏ Evaluating/analyzing/appraising
- ❏ Managing time and priorities
- ❏ Managing resources efficiently
- ❏ Establishing systems/procedures
- ❏ Demonstrating follow-through

Your Skills

The next dimension involves looking at your skills. You can also think of these as your abilities, talents, gifts, or competencies. Skills are what you use in your life and in a career to accomplish things, to reach certain goals or ends. Skills enable you to reach those things you consider valuable.

As you consider what your skills are, think especially about ones that can be transferred from one job to another. For example, you may have edited a high school newspaper and organized a small staff of three in doing so. The transferable skills that you learned from that job include interviewing, writing, editing, organizing people, and leading. These skills can be applied in any number of careers or roles you may be considering, whether that career involves newspaper editing, sales, politics, running a business, or work in the social sciences.

A note about type: As you exercise your type preferences, it is likely that you will naturally develop some skills over others. For example, people who prefer Judging may be more inclined than people who prefer Perceiving to develop organizing skills. However, people who prefer Perceiving can develop excellent skills in organizing. They may, however, be less interested in doing so, or they may be less satisfied in a career that

requires them to constantly use their organizing skills. Remember also that skills can be learned and developed with practice; hence you don't have to be limited by lack of skill in an area.

Skills also provide additional information whether they appear to be consistent or inconsistent with your type preferences. For example, an Introvert who has more skills (and interests) in working with people may be more satisfied in a career in teaching, whereas an Introvert who has more skills (and interests) in technical data-oriented areas may be more satisfied in a career in computer and information sciences.

Look at the skills list on the previous page to identify areas where you have—or would like to develop—skill. Be honest with yourself.

At the bottom of this page, write which skills are the most important to you and which appear reasonably well developed. You may also want to write down skills that you would like to develop. Also note that you may have developed some skills that you are not particularly interested in using in future careers or roles.

After you have written down these skills, consider what they mean for your career exploration? You might find it helpful to talk about these skills with someone else.

Skills Checklist II

In the spaces provided, list other skills you have that were not listed.

☐ _____   ☐ _____

☐ _____   ☐ _____

☐ _____   ☐ _____

☐ _____   ☐ _____

☐ _____   ☐ _____

☐ _____   ☐ _____

YOUR SKILLS. *Write your highest skills in the following spaces. How does this information add to or clarify your understanding of yourself, potential work settings, and careers you may be considering? How might you pursue them? You may also want to discuss these with someone else.*

_____

_____

_____

_____

_____

_____

_____

_____

_____

_____

_____

_____

_____

_____

_____

_____

_____

_____

_____

_____

_____

_____

_____

_____

_____

_____

To learn more about careers that are linked to your values, interests, and skills, you might want to visit a Web site administered and sponsored by the Department of Labor's Employment and Training Administration (www.onetcenter.org). The O*NET Project provides assessment resources and occupational information. The Online Center link (http://online.onetcenter.org) lets you look up the specifics of the occupations in the database, and read detailed summaries of skills, knowledge, interests, and activities for each. You can also browse for occupations based on knowledge, interests, skills, values, and industry.

Looking at Your Type Dynamics and Development

At this point, you've gained some understanding of who you are by exploring your type, values, interests, and skills. We now return to type for another dimension in your self-understanding: your type dynamics and type development.

Your Type Dynamics: One Key in Determining What Appeals to You

The four functions are the building blocks of your type. Everyone needs and uses the four basic mental functions: Sensing, Intuition, Thinking, and Feeling. People simply prefer to focus on some rather than others, and prefer them in a particular order. This is what is meant when we refer to *type dynamics*. The type table in this section shows the order of preference each of the sixteen types has for the four functions: Sensing, Intuition, Thinking, and Feeling.

One of the two middle letters of your type is your *favorite* function (also called your *dominant*). Look at the following chart (page 18) to see which is your favorite. When you are doing work that uses your favorite function, you tend to feel the most competent and sure of yourself, and you will likely experience the work as easier and more natural.

The other of the two middle letters of your type is your *second favorite* function (also called the *auxiliary*). This function tends to be the second most well developed and lends balance to your dominant function. Work that uses your second favorite function also tends to be experienced as easier and more natural.

Since your dominant and auxiliary functions are your most-preferred functions, and usually the most well developed, they tend to be *the most* important as you think about career exploration. They can give you insight into what you may find motivating in a career, what roles and tasks may appeal to you, and what skills you will most easily develop. For example, if Intuition (N) and Feeling (F) are your two most-favored functions, then you will probably be more inclined to focus on the possibilities, the future, and have concern for harmony with others. As a result, you might find it relatively easy to develop skills in working with symbols or skills in working with people. NFs are indeed often found in such careers (e.g., the arts, counseling, writing) and are drawn to tasks or roles that draw on these qualities (e.g., coaching and mentoring, providing service, communicating with or motivating others).

You might also have more difficulty or less interest in developing skills that use your Sensing and Thinking functions, because these are the *opposites* of your natural preferences. NFs are found much less often in careers that draw on the qualities often associated with Sensing and Thinking (e.g., management, police work, accounting), and they are also less drawn to tasks and roles that use those functions (e.g., organizing and retrieving data, roles where they must compete with or impersonally analyze other people).

If **SENSING** is your dominant or auxiliary, you may tend to find appealing those roles and tasks that draw on these qualities: Attention to detail; trust in experience; data provided by the five senses; applications of methods to pragmatic concerns

If **INTUITION** is your dominant or auxiliary, you may tend to find appealing those roles and tasks that draw on these qualities: Attention to meaning, patterns, and possibilities; brainstorming; considering long-term implications; dealing with theory and abstract ideas

If **THINKING** is your dominant or auxiliary, you may tend to find appealing those roles and tasks that draw on these qualities: Logical and impersonal analysis; investigating how something works and/or how to solve a problem; seeking understanding and increasing effectiveness

If **FEELING** is your dominant or auxiliary, you may tend to find appealing those roles and tasks that draw on these qualities: Weighing what is good for people and being concerned with ethical Issues; consideration of the people side of problems; demonstrating sensitivity and empathy

Priorities of Functions

ISTJ	ISFJ	INFJ	INTJ
1) Sensing$_I$ (Dominant)	1) Sensing$_I$ (Dominant)	1) Intuition$_I$ (Dominant)	1) Intuition$_I$ (Dominant)
2) Thinking$_E$ (Auxiliary)	2) Feeling$_E$ (Auxiliary)	2) Feeling$_E$ (Auxiliary)	2) Thinking$_E$ (Auxiliary)
3) Feeling$_{E-I}$ (Tertiary)	3) Thinking$_{E-I}$ (Tertiary)	3) Thinking$_{E-I}$ (Tertiary)	3) Feeling$_{E-I}$ (Tertiary)
4) Intuition$_E$ (Inferior)	4) Intuition$_E$ (Inferior)	4) Sensing$_E$ (Inferior)	4) Sensing$_E$ (Inferior)

ISTP	ISFP	INFP	INTP
1) Thinking$_I$ (Dominant)	1) Feeling$_I$ (Dominant)	1) Feeling$_I$ (Dominant)	1) Thinking$_I$ (Dominant)
2) Sensing$_E$ (Auxiliary)	2) Sensing$_E$ (Auxiliary)	2) Intuition$_E$ (Auxiliary)	2) Intuition$_E$ (Auxiliary)
3) Intuition$_{E-I}$ (Tertiary)	3) Intuition$_{E-I}$ (Tertiary)	3) Sensing$_{E-I}$ (Tertiary)	3) Sensing$_{E-I}$ (Tertiary)
4) Feeling$_E$ (Inferior)	4) Thinking$_E$ (Inferior)	4) Thinking$_E$ (Inferior)	4) Feeling$_E$ (Inferior)

ESTP	ESFP	ENFP	ENTP
1) Sensing$_E$ (Dominant)	1) Sensing$_E$ (Dominant)	1) Intuition$_E$ (Dominant)	1) Intuition$_E$ (Dominant)
2) Thinking$_I$ (Auxiliary)	2) Feeling$_I$ (Auxiliary)	2) Feeling$_I$ (Auxiliary)	2) Thinking$_I$ (Auxiliary)
3) Feeling$_{E-I}$ (Tertiary)	3) Thinking$_{E-I}$ (Tertiary)	3) Thinking$_{E-I}$ (Tertiary)	3) Feeling$_{E-I}$ (Tertiary)
4) Intuition$_I$ (Inferior)	4) Intuition$_I$ (Inferior)	4) Sensing$_I$ (Inferior)	4) Sensing$_I$ (Inferior)

ESTJ	ESFJ	ENFJ	ENTJ
1) Thinking$_E$ (Dominant)	1) Feeling$_E$ (Dominant)	1) Feeling$_E$ (Dominant)	1) Thinking$_E$ (Dominant)
2) Sensing$_I$ (Auxiliary)	2) Sensing$_I$ (Auxiliary)	2) Intuition$_I$ (Auxiliary)	2) Intuition$_I$ (Auxiliary)
3) Intuition$_{E-I}$ (Tertiary)	3) Intuition$_{E-I}$ (Tertiary)	3) Sensing$_{E-I}$ (Tertiary)	3) Sensing$_{E-I}$ (Tertiary)
4) Feeling$_I$ (Inferior)	4) Thinking$_I$ (Inferior)	4) Thinking$_I$ (Inferior)	4) Feeling$_I$ (Inferior)

E = Extraverted   I = Introverted   E–I = Theorists differ on the orientation of the tertiary

Extraverts use their dominant function in their Extraverted world, which is where they prefer to focus their attention. If you are, for example, an ENFP that means you like to apply your Intuition to the outer world of people and things. For balance, Extraverts develop their auxiliary function (second favorite) for use in their Introverted world. An ENFP likes to use the Feeling function in the inner world of ideas, thus their Feeling function is not as readily seen by others. *Introverts* use their dominant function in the inner world of the mind, which is where they prefer to focus attention. If you are an ISTJ, for example, you prefer to use your Sensing function in the inner world of ideas. For balance, Introverts develop their auxiliary function (second favorite) for use in their Extraverted world. An ISTJ likes to use their Thinking function to organize the outer world of people and things.

Your least-preferred function tends to be your least well-developed function. It is also called your *inferior* function because it tends to lag behind all of the others in its development. It is the opposite function of your dominant function, and is oriented in the opposite direction from your dominant function. For example, if Extraverted Feeling were your dominant function (as it is for ESFJs and ENFJs), Introverted Thinking would be your fourth or least well-developed function.

Your least-preferred function provides you with clues to areas of your life that you tend to avoid, and involves skills that interest you the least or that you may have more difficulty developing. Work that draws on this function is often experienced as boring, difficult, or tiring. For example, if Introverted Thinking were your least favorite function, you might tend to avoid tasks that require a great deal of impersonal analysis of data, a critical or detached approach to people, or quiet and inwardly focused problem solving (e.g., as in the theoretical or applied sciences, statistics, economics).

While stretching to use your least-preferred modes is valuable and good, you may want to pursue careers or roles that allow you to use your dominant and auxiliary functions rather than those that require you to constantly use your least-preferred function. If you are drawn to—or find yourself in—a career or role that does require you to use your least-preferred function a great deal, then consider the following. How might you revise your approach, redefine or change your role, or refocus on different aspects of the job so that you also get to use your dominant and auxiliary functions as well? To gain a deeper understanding of when and how you might consider the role of your third and least-preferred functions in your career development and management, review the next section: "Your Type Development."

Look at the priorities of functions chart on page 18 and note which are the dominant (favorite), auxiliary (second favorite) and least-preferred functions for your type. What role might these functions play in your career choice? What kind of career areas, tasks, or roles might be easier (and more interesting) or more difficult (and less interesting) for you based on what you know of these functions? Make some notes on the worksheet on the following page.

MY TYPE DYNAMICS

Look at the Priorities of Functions chart on page 18, and note your favorite, second favorite, and least favorite functions. Also note whether you orient these to the inner (Introverted) world or outer (Extraverted) world.

My dominant (favorite) function is _____ *and I orient it to the (inner or outer)* _____ *world.*

Career areas, tasks, or roles that might be more interesting based on my favorite function:

_____

_____

_____

_____

_____

_____

_____

My auxiliary (second favorite) function is _____ *and I orient it to the (inner or outer)* _____ *world.*

Career areas, tasks, or roles that might be more interesting based on my second favorite function:

_____

_____

_____

_____

_____

_____

_____

My least-preferred (inferior) function is _____ *and I orient it to the (inner or outer)* _____ *world.*

Career areas, tasks, or roles that might be less interesting based on my least-preferred function:

_____

_____

_____

_____

_____

_____

_____

Your Type Development

Individuals tend to develop the four functions in a relatively predictable order through their lives. Since the order of development is also the order of preference for the functions, the type table on page 18 also shows you the order in which you tend to develop the four functions throughout your life. This order can also play an important role in your career development.

Insight into how your career interests can change across time

Why is type development important for your career exploration? As you move through life, your values, interests, and skills change and broaden. This is partially due to your development of the four functions. As you begin to see how the functions are being developed in your life, you can gain some understanding of your individual needs and changing career options. Because your functions develop over a lifetime, your career values and interests may be different at midlife than they were when you were in high school. Your dominant and auxiliary functions will always be your favorite functions, but the career options you consider may broaden in later life as you develop your tertiary function, and possibly your least-preferred function.

Since no career lets us spend 100 percent of the time using just our favorite and second favorite functions, we have to stretch at times to use our tertiary and least-preferred functions. This stretching is good for our development, but too much stretching can be discouraging. Careers that require you to primarily use your third and least-preferred function may leave you feeling stressed and drained. This will depend somewhat on your stage of type development, but you will always want to make use of your dominant and auxiliary functions in some way, regardless of your stage of development. Think back on school subjects you have studied or jobs that you have had. Which energized you and which drained you?

For example, if you are an ISFP, you will probably find a satisfying career that makes use of your dominant Feeling and auxiliary Sensing functions. Thus, you are more likely to enjoy

and feel competent in a career in which you can make use of your deep concern for people and harmony, your attention to the richness of sensory information, and your hands-on learning style. You are less likely to find satisfying a career that *primarily* relies on your least-preferred function of Thinking or your tertiary function of Intuition. Thus, although you may be happy in a career where you can solve problems to directly help others, you may end up feeling stressed and drained if you are in a career that constantly asks you to solve abstract, scientific, or business management problems that require a more impersonal and analytical problem-solving approach.

If you are at a stage in your life when you are experiencing the need to develop and make use of your tertiary function, you may want to consider a career that will challenge you to develop the skills of that function, or possibly even your fourth function. For example, if you are an ISFP who is closer to midlife, you may want to consider a career or consider expanding your current career in a way that allows you to make greater use of your tertiary Intuition, or even your least-preferred Thinking function. That is, you might feel the need to focus more on abstract possibilities, theories and symbols, and even feel the excitement of using your Thinking function to solve problems from a more objective analytical framework; for instance, you might find yourself newly enjoying games that involve strategy and logic.

Take some time to think about your stage of life and development and reflect on what roles your dominant and auxiliary functions play (or could play) in your life and work, and use the space provided to make notes about your thoughts.

Are you primarily making use of your dominant and auxiliary? Are you at a stage where you want to pursue a career, or make a change within a career where you will be challenged to make use of your tertiary or least-preferred functions? Can you fulfill the needs of your tertiary and least-preferred functions outside of your career (in a hobby for example)? You may also find it helpful to talk about type dynamics and development with someone who knows type.

Environments (e.g., family, culture) sometimes discourage individuals from developing their favorite functions, or push them to develop functions two, three, or four earlier than they normally would be interested in doing so. If you read a description of your type and it seems surprisingly on target for you, start with the expectation that your development has been on your natural path. If you aren't sure, take your doubts seriously, and explore other possibilities by reading different type descriptions and continuing to explore which preferences seem most natural for you.

YOUR DOMINANT AND AUXILIARY. *What roles do your dominant and auxiliary functions play (or could play) in your life and work?*

_____
_____
_____
_____
_____
_____

What Do I Want?

Now that you've done some assessment of your values, interests, skills, and work environment preferences, and now that you know a bit more about the dynamics of your type, it's a good time to consider the following questions.

What do I want in my career? What do I really want? Remember, there's much more to your career direction than your type preferences. So in responding to the questions, consider all of who you are—not simply your type. Also, you don't have to have a specific career title or job in mind; you can just respond based on what you've learned about yourself so far. For example, what kinds of things do you like to do? What tasks and roles appeal to you? What skills do you want to use? What kind of environment do you want to work in? Make some notes here.

It's valuable to consider these questions before you read your type description in section 2. Then, after you've read your type description, you may want to revisit these questions and respond to them again.

WHAT DO I WANT? *What kinds of things do you like to do? What tasks and roles appeal to you? What skills do you want to use? What kind of environment do you want to work in?*

_____
_____
_____
_____
_____
_____

Looking at Careers

The type descriptions in this section are intended to provide you with information for your career exploration, development, and management, not to encourage or discourage you in a given career pursuit.

Career research shows that type preferences are indeed linked to career choice—that is, different personality types choose some careers more often than they choose others. In the type descriptions, we've indicated what some of those patterns are. The careers listed with each type description are intended to *suggest* patterns of interest for each type, and to provide you with specific career ideas you may not have yet considered. They are *not* intended to be a list of careers that would absolutely be "right" for you. Please be aware also that not all careers and occupations are represented in these lists.

Research shows that virtually *every type is found in every career* and that using your personality type as the *primary* information in making a career decision is not the key to satisfaction and success. Many different personality types can be successful and happy in the same career. We also know that different types are often drawn to very different aspects, specialties, or roles within the same career.

In exploring your career options and in managing your career, give the *most* weight to your interests, values, skills, life goals, and lifestyle needs. Be sure to gather information about yourself using tools designed specifically for the assessment of career interests and skills—the lists in the previous sections of this booklet are designed just for that purpose. You can use the career patterns of the types to generate other options you might not have yet considered.

Most importantly, use knowledge of your type to recognize how you might approach all the different things you need to do to build your career (e.g., networking, information gathering, decision making, and job search) and which roles and tasks might appeal to you *within* any given career.

In summary, identify *what you* want in a career through self-examination and through the variety of career questionnaires that are available, learn about *who you* are at a very individual level, and then use knowledge of your type to clarify how you can find, create and/or carve out a niche that meets your career aspirations and sense of self.

Career Choices Where Your Type is Less Frequent

Since people are drawn to careers for many reasons other than their type, individuals of a given type are certainly found in the careers on their "less attractive" list—that is, careers where their type is less frequent.

As you clarify *what you want* in a career, using *all* that you know about yourself, you may find yourself drawn to a field that seems to be less frequented by people with your type preferences. You might then ask yourself some of the following questions.

- Will I be called on to use a type preference that may not be as well developed for me?

- Am I willing to develop (or have I already developed) the skills of those preferences?

- Am I at the point in my life when using my nonpreferences might be interesting and appealing?

- As an unusual type within that career, how might I take a different approach that can make a valuable or innovative contribution to the field?

- Is there a niche, path, or role within that career that would allow me to make use of my preferences?

If you find yourself already in a field or a job that seems to be less frequented by people with your type preferences, you have several options to consider. You can certainly consider a career or job change. However, there may be many good reasons why you want to be where you are, including having chosen this career based on your interests, skills, and values. In that case, you might consider some of the following suggestions.

- Find, cultivate, or create a niche or specialty for yourself where you *do* get to use your preferences in a way that meets your needs.

- Find an environment and/or colleagues with whom you *do* share some personality qualities.

- Modify *what* and *how* you do your work so that you are taking on tasks that *do* fit for your personality style.

- Consider especially how you will ensure that your Extravert or Introvert needs will get met if you're in a job or environment that requires you to behave opposite to your preference for long periods.

TYPE DESCRIPTIONS
FOR CAREER DEVELOPMENT
AND EXPLORATION

ISTJ	ISFJ	INFJ	INTJ
ISTP	ISFP	INFP	INTP
ESTP	ESFP	ENFP	ENTP
ESTJ	ESFJ	ENFJ	ENTJ

ISTJ

Summary Career Description

ISTJs are most likely to find interesting and satisfying those careers that make use of their depth of concentration, their reliance on facts, their use of logic and analysis, and their ability to organize. ISTJs are very often found in management careers, particularly in the areas of government, public service, and private business, and they are often found in technical and production-oriented careers as well. Their task orientation, realistic grounding, dependability, and respect for the facts often draw them to careers or jobs that call for organized approaches to data, people, or things.

Overall Style

ISTJs have patience and dedication that is often communicated to those around them as a calm composure, thus they often bring stability to the work environment. As a result they can engender a degree of trust in others that leads to placement in management or supervisory positions for the ISTJs that require the overseeing of practical matters. In addition, their dedication can make them difficult to distract or discourage from a given task, an orientation that leads to thoroughness and accuracy in work. They will also painstakingly follow through on commitments they make. ISTJs are exceptionally practical and though they may not always agree with the goals of a work setting or institution, they do find a comfort in structure and will guarantee that procedures are followed.

Appealing Environments, Tasks, Roles

ISTJs are often found in environments or roles where realistic precision and technical know-how are required. They are also drawn to tasks and arenas where detailed knowledge is required and where the work involves practical or hands-on experience. ISTJs report being attracted to career environments where there is some structure, where the demands and rewards are clear, where they can take on responsibilities, and where they can work to gain status and security. In addition, they enjoy working alone, and if they must work with groups they tend to prefer smaller ones; they also like being able to prepare projects or group presentations ahead of time. ISTJs want results from their work that are tangible, and they will work to perfect the efficient delivery of a service or product. They are often found in, and drawn to, management roles.

Job Search Style

For ISTJs the job search tends to be a thoughtful and practical process. They are excellent gatherers of job-related information, and they can be very organized and thorough in preparing application materials or in marketing themselves. Their dependability and willingness to take on responsibility will usually be communicated to others during the job search.

Potential drawbacks for ISTJs in the job search may include a tendency to narrow the search too much, failure to consider unusual opportunities or job options, and a tendency to be cautious and to undersell themselves. Under stress, ISTJs may become pessimistic during this process, and they may also become uncharacteristically impulsive. They may find it useful to engage their ability to be objective, and to see the importance of developing some flexibility in their interactions with others. They may also benefit from developing a healthy amount of enthusiasm and assertiveness as they engage in the job search.

Career Areas: More Attractive

People with ISTJ preferences are often attracted to careers and occupations in the following areas:

- Engineering: industrial, petroleum, environmental, nuclear

- Engineering: civil, mechanical

- Military

- Finance, banking, accounting

- Manufacturing and production

- Aviation: pilot

- Trades: mechanics, electronics

- Management: small business and production

- Management: office and executive

- Law enforcement and other protective services

- Economics

- Computer science, data analysis, mathematics

- Dentistry

- Nursing and healthcare administration

- Construction

- Purchasing

- Management and supervision: building, construction, agriculture

- Educational administration

- Teaching: trades, technical, math

But ISTJs can find satisfaction and success in entirely different areas than those listed here. The key to *getting where one wants to go* involves first identifying what one *really* wants—something that comes from a more individual place than type. Individuals with ISTJ preferences then need to use knowledge of their type to gain insight into how they might approach the different activities involved in planning a career. In other words, ISTJs need to build on the strengths of their type and address potential obstacles that may come along with their style as they explore options, connect with others, make decisions, and manage their careers.

Career Areas: Less Attractive

Remember, every type is in virtually every career. People with ISTJ preferences are, however, less often attracted to careers and occupations in art, graphic design, music, photography, sales/advertising, and personal care and service. They are also typically found less often in careers characterized by a great deal of nurturing work and/or relationship-oriented work, or careers that require a significant amount of spontaneous adaptation or expressiveness in a group context.

ISTJs who find themselves in—or drawn to—a career in which their type seems to be less frequent may want to read "Career Choices Where Your Type is Less Frequent" on page 24.

Summary Career Description

ISFJs are most likely to find interesting and satisfying those careers that make use of their depth of concentration, their reliance on facts, their warmth and sympathy (i.e., their emphasis on interpersonal values), and their ability to organize. ISFJs are very often found in careers that involve nurturing or healing others and also in some spiritually oriented careers. Their sense of duty, personal commitment, and practicality often draw them to careers in which they can support and be of service to others. These same qualities can also lead to their effectiveness in the helping and health-oriented careers.

Overall Style

Their loyalty and respect for tradition often helps create a feeling of stability in the work environment around them. In addition, their quiet warmth and tact are clearly felt by others even as they attend to their work, ensuring that organizational or work goals are met. Their willingness to take on responsibility is grounded in a very personal conclusion that the job is worth doing and is of benefit to others; they are typically exceptionally dependable. Once they have dedicated themselves to a job, they tend to carry it all the way through until it is done. Their pragmatism and sense of order often lead them to careers where they need to impose or maintain order on a body of information (e.g., a library) or some setting (e.g., an office). ISFJs do appreciate a degree of structure and organization in their work, and they are often found working behind the scenes ensuring that things are running smoothly.

Appealing Environments, Tasks, Roles

ISFJs are often found in environments or roles where they can draw on their characteristic quiet warmth and concern for others, as well as on their capacity for precision and painstaking attention to detail. They are also drawn to tasks and arenas that require direct personal care of others, attention to others' physical or spiritual well-being, and/or require some technical knowledge. ISFJs report being attracted to career environments where they can be of help to others or provide some form of practical service to others, where they can take on responsibility and organize what they do, and where they can see tangible results from their work. In addition, they typically enjoy working in environments that are stable, where they can make pragmatic use of their attention to detail, and where they can focus attention fully on a project or person. At times ISFJs do need a place or space where they can work alone in an uninterrupted fashion, and when they do work with others they prefer working one-to-one rather than with larger groups of people.

Job Search Style

For ISFJs the job search tends to be a very thoughtful and practical process. They are excellent gatherers of job-related information, and can be very thorough and organized in their job search, job application, or in marketing themselves. Their perseverance, stability, and warmth are usually communicated to others during the job search. Potential drawbacks for ISFJs in the job search may include a tendency to overlook unusual job possibilities or options, a tendency to undersell themselves, and sensitivity to rejection. Under stress, ISFJs may feel some pessimism during this process, and they may become uncharacteristically impulsive. They can benefit from discussing their concerns with a trusted friend and from seeing the importance of developing a larger perspective on their situation. They may also benefit from cultivating a healthy amount of assertiveness and optimism as they go about the job search.

Career Areas: More Attractive

People with ISFJ preferences are often attracted to careers and occupations in the following areas:

- Nursing: registered, licensed practical
- Teaching: pre-k through elementary and other
- Religious professions
- Medical technology
- Medicine: family and general practice
- Veterinary medicine
- Dental hygiene
- Health education and services
- Social services and social work
- Library and information service professions
- Physical therapy
- Dietician and nutritional specialist
- Bookkeeping and bank teller
- Social service administration
- Personal services: trainer, cosmetology
- Corrections and probation
- Secretary and administrative assistant
- Office support, data entry, word processing
- Hotel, motel, lodging manager, and clerk
- Paralegal

But ISFJs can find satisfaction and success in entirely different areas than those listed here. The key to *getting where one wants to go* involves first identifying what one *really* wants—something that comes from a more individual place than type. Individuals with ISFJ preferences then need to use knowledge of their type to gain insight into how they might approach the different activities involved in planning a career. In other words, ISFJs need to build on the strengths of their type and address potential obstacles that may come along with their style as they explore options, connect with others, make decisions, and manage their careers.

Career Areas: Less Attractive

Remember, every type is in virtually every career. People with ISFJ preferences are, however, less often attracted to careers and occupations in: economics, marketing and sales, engineering, psychology, architecture, law, and administration in such tough-minded fields as military and protective services. They are also typically found less often in careers characterized by a great deal of analytically oriented technical work or a distant analytical approach to people, work that requires ongoing attention to more theoretical and symbolic information, or careers that require continual adaptation and frequent change.

ISFJs who find themselves in—or drawn to—a career in which their type seems to be less frequent may want to read "Career Choices Where Your Type is Less Frequent" on page 24.

INFJ

Summary Career Description

INFJs are most likely to find interesting and satisfying those careers that make use of their depth of concentration, their grasp of possibilities, their warmth and sympathy (i.e., their emphasis on interpersonal values), and their ability to organize. INFJs are very often found in careers where creativity and tending to human development are primary activities. Their orientation to people, their confidence in their insights into the nature of things and people, and their fertile imagination often attract them to careers in the arts and careers where they can draw out the possibilities in others—as in religious, therapeutic, and teaching professions.

Overall Style

Their intense inner vision, ability to establish harmonious relationships with others, and their skills in written and oral communication can often draw others into supporting their goals. As a result, INFJs are often called on to provide leadership in areas that involve attending to the physical, emotional, and/or spiritual needs of others. INFJs are full of idealism and lofty goals, and though not always apparent, they are intensely individualistic and private persons. They are also particularly attracted to careers that provide opportunities for philosophical reflection, and are attracted to careers where they have the opportunity to grow as well.

Appealing Environments, Tasks, Roles

INFJs are often found in environments or roles where human contact and comfort with abstraction, symbols, and the imagination are required. They are also drawn to tasks and arenas in which spiritual themes or artistic expression are involved or where they can use their often exceptional empathic abilities. INFJs report being attracted to career environments where they can work with people to empower them and facilitate growth, where they can be creative and innovative, where they feel they are doing something consistent with their values, and where they can be independent and autonomous. In addition they enjoy challenges, and value the opportunity to express themselves and see the results of their vision. Although they value harmonious relations with others and they are oriented to helping people develop, INFJs definitely need a significant amount of alone time in their work, which allows them to focus on the inner world of ideas and images.

Job Search Style

For INFJs the job search can be an opportunity to use creativity, as well as organizational and rapport-building skills. They can envision job possibilities easily, and can pursue them both through their ability to connect with others and through their potential ability to be task oriented. Their interpersonal orientation, persuasiveness, and insight are usually communicated to others during the job search. Potential drawbacks for INFJs in the job search include unrealistic expectations for a job, inaction, painful feelings that the job search is grueling or cheapening, and inattention to details of jobs or of the job search. Under stress, INFJs may develop a potentially adversarial attitude toward the world of work and may get caught up in less relevant details. They may find it helpful to maintain a sense of humor as they view events from a broader, more meaningful perspective and as they develop more realistic job expectations and flexibility in dealing with the details of the job search.

Career Areas: More Attractive

People with INFJ preferences are often attracted to careers and occupations in the following areas:

- Religious professions
- Teaching: middle, high school, university
- Writing
- Performing arts: music, singing, composing, directing
- Fine arts, graphic design, multimedia artist
- Psychology: clinical, counseling, educational
- Counseling and psychotherapy
- Occupational therapy
- Research
- Medicine: family practice, psychiatry, pathology, surgery
- Physician's assistant
- Dental hygiene
- Architecture
- Interior design
- Marketing
- Social sciences
- Educational consulting
- Vocational education
- Librarian, information sciences
- Engineering: biomedical, petroleum
- Environmental sciences

But INFJs can find satisfaction and success in entirely different areas than those listed here. The key to *getting where one wants to go* involves first identifying what one *really* wants—something that comes from a more individual place than type. Individuals with INFJ preferences then need to use knowledge of their type to gain insight into how they might approach the different activities involved in planning a career. In other words, INFJs need to build on the strengths of their type and address potential obstacles that may come along with their style as they explore options, connect with others, make decisions, and manage their careers.

Career Areas: Less Attractive

Every type is in virtually every career, and clearly people are drawn to careers for many reasons other than their type. People with INFJ preferences are, however, less often attracted to careers and occupations in the military, corrections and protective services, construction and production, and finance/accounting. They are also typically found less often in careers characterized by a great deal of technical work, attention to detail, work that requires realistic precision or production, mechanical work, work that requires more bureaucratic management abilities, or work that may involve a significant amount of interpersonal conflict.

INFJs who find themselves in—or drawn to—a career in which their type seems to be less frequent may want to read "Career Choices Where Your Type is Less Frequent" on page 24.

INTJ

Summary Career Description

INTJs are most likely to find interesting and satisfying those careers that make use of their depth of concentration, their grasp of possibilities, their use of logic and analysis, and their ability to organize. INTJs are often found in academic, scientific, theoretical, and technical positions that allow or require tough-minded analysis and periods of solitary concentration. Their task orientation, powers of abstraction, perseverance, and willingness to look at situations or systems in creative ways often draw them to careers where they can pursue the implementation of an inner vision and/or create new systems. Their creativity may also find expression in artistic endeavors or careers in the arts.

Overall Style

Autonomy and individual achievement are extremely important to INTJs, and they are not easily deflected from a task or goal on which they have set their minds. They prefer challenge and appreciate opportunities to apply their creativity and intuitive insights, as well as chances to expand their repertoire of skills. Though not always seen, INTJs experience a strong need to engage in quiet, even philosophical reflection, prior to engaging the external tasks of their chosen field of work. Their trust in their own insights, their faith that they see into the meaning behind events, and their willingness to bring their insights into practical real-world application often communicate to others an impression of confidence. Though these qualities often lead to their being placed in executive and management positions, INTJs are intensely individualistic and resist being bound to routine.

Appealing Environments, Tasks, Roles

INTJs are often found in environments or roles where creativity and/or technical know-how are required. They are also drawn to tasks and arenas where planning, revising, or designing for the future are involved. INTJs report being attracted to career environments where they can be independent and creative, think systemically, feel challenged, and believe that their work makes a difference. They pursue competence and mastery, and often will move quickly to something else once they have gained a sufficient level of some skill or knowledge. Consequently, whatever career they choose must have opportunities for learning. INTJs need time to work alone, and when they work with others, they hope and expect those persons will be skilled and competent as well.

Job Search Style

For INTJs the job search is an opportunity to use their creativity, their skills in synthesizing information, and their ability to approach the market in an organized and strategic fashion. They can usually envision many career possibilities, and can selectively target and pursue job options with their potential ability to be task oriented. Their competence, analytical skills, and insight are usually communicated to others during the job search. Potential drawbacks for INTJs in the job search include unrealistic expectations for a job, inaction, failure to communicate warmth or diplomacy in interactions with others, and inattention to details of jobs or of the job search. Under stress, INTJs may develop a potentially adversarial attitude toward the world of work and may get caught up in less relevant details. They may find it helpful to analyze their experience objectively when they see the need to be more realistic in their expectations about jobs and to be more flexible in dealing with the details of the job search.

Career Areas: More Attractive

People with INTJ preferences are often attracted to careers and occupations in the following areas:

- Physical, life, and social sciences
- Law: lawyer, judge
- Executive and manager: sciences, architecture, legal
- Computer sciences
- Economics
- Executive and manager: military, protective services
- Management consulting
- Human resources
- Engineering: nuclear, electrical, aeronautical, computer, materials
- Psychology: clinical, industrial, organizational
- Social services
- Executive and manager: education, community, social services
- Urban planning
- Arts and entertainment: actor, musician, composer
- Photography
- Multimedia arts and design
- Teaching: university
- Research
- Writing, editing, journalism
- Medicine: internal, pathology, research

But INTJs can find satisfaction and success in entirely different areas than those listed here. The key to *getting where one wants to go* involves first identifying what one *really* wants—something that comes from a more individual place than type. Individuals with INTJ preferences then need to use knowledge of their type to gain insight into how they might approach the different activities involved in planning a career. In other words, INTJs need to build on the strengths of their type and address potential obstacles that may come along with their style as they explore options, connect with others, make decisions, and manage their careers.

Career Areas: Less Attractive

Every type is in virtually every career, and clearly people are drawn to careers for many reasons other than their type. People with INTJ preferences are, however, less often attracted to careers and occupations in sales, office administration, personal care and services, health-care support, food preparation and service, and construction. They are also typically found less often in careers characterized by a great deal of nurturing work; relationship-oriented work; work that requires practical, routine production or delivery of services; or careers that depend predominantly on hands-on work, attention to detail, and/or adherence to structures imposed by others.

INTJs who find themselves in—or drawn to—a career in which their type seems to be less frequent may want to read "Career Choices Where Your Type is Less Frequent" on page 24.

Summary Career Description

ISTPs are most likely to find interesting and satisfying those careers that make use of their depth of concentration, their reliance on facts, their use of logic and analysis, and their adaptability. ISTPs are found in a variety of careers, but are most often found in ones that require a tough-minded analytical and realistic approach. Many of these careers are related to building and production, while others involve providing direct delivery of technically oriented services. Their quiet adaptability, realistic grounding, and their willingness to critically analyze the facts often draw them to careers where they can take a pragmatic approach to problem solving and troubleshooting.

Overall Style

Their keen powers of observation and their desire for a wealth of hands-on and sensory experiences often lead ISTPs to develop exceptionally high levels of skill with the tools or instruments they choose to use, whether that tool is a computer, a hammer, a spreadsheet, or a sailboat. Consequently, ISTPs are often found in fields that require a craftsmanlike approach; and if the field is more scientific, they are often found in the more applied aspects of the field. They may also manifest a great curiosity about things, not so much in an abstract search for their meaning, but a curiosity about how and why they work and about their application. They often enjoy jobs that involve a measure of adventure, though they may choose to meet that need outside of their work life. ISTPs also tend to resist too much structure.

Appealing Environments, Tasks, Roles

ISTPs are often found in environments or roles where precision and technical know-how are required. They are also drawn to tasks and arenas where mechanical understanding plays an important part, or to careers where they can use logical analysis to make sense of a variety of facts and real-world problems. They are often quite skilled at making the most effective use of what is actually available, and they may make very good troubleshooters. ISTPs report being attracted to career environments that are fun, where they can make use of their grasp of the details, where there is intellectual stimulation, where there are tangible results from their work, or where they can respond and adapt to what is happening in the present. They are also drawn to outdoor activities and/or careers that provide them with some excitement. They need time alone, are not particularly inclined to supervise others, and often choose jobs where they can work independently.

Job Search Style

For ISTPs the job search is an opportunity to apply their analytical skills to the facts of the job search. They can pragmatically gather information on prospective jobs, and critically look at what they need to do to apply for a job or to market themselves. Their ability to adapt to the needs of the moment, take risks, and think realistically about problems are usually communicated to others during the job search. Potential drawbacks for ISTPs during the job search include a tendency to focus on the immediate present rather than on long-term job plans, difficulty in following through with job search tasks, and putting off making job decisions out of fear that something more exciting may come along. Under stress, ISTPs can feel overwhelmed as they engage in this process, and can benefit from checking the facts and realities of their situation. They can also benefit from considering what is truly of value to them, which will give them the drive to persevere and follow through on all parts of the job search.

Career Areas: More Attractive

People with ISTP preferences are often attracted to careers and occupations in the following areas:

- Forestry

- Agriculture and plant sciences

- Farming and ranching

- Construction and trades: carpentry, electrical, other

- Military

- Aviation: air crew, assembler, mechanic

- Engine and equipment mechanic

- Engineering: electrical, mechanical, computer hardware and software

- Electrical, electronics, telecommunications installation, and repair

- Geology and geophysics

- Protective services: law enforcement, corrections

- Computer sciences: systems administrator, operator

- Surveying

- Machinist

- Power and chemical plant operations

- Law: lawyer, legal administration

- Physical therapy

- Accounting

- Manager and administrator: small business, government, social services

- Teaching: adult education, coaching

But ISTPs can find satisfaction and success in entirely different areas than those listed here. The key to *getting where one wants to go* involves first identifying what one *really* wants—something that comes from a more individual place than type. Individuals with ISTP preferences then need to use knowledge of their type to gain insight into how they might approach the different activities involved in planning a career. In other words, ISTPs need to build on the strengths of their type and address potential obstacles that may come along with

their style as they explore options, connect with others, make decisions, and manage their careers.

Career Areas: Less Attractive

Every type is in virtually every career, and clearly people are drawn to careers for many reasons other than their type. People with ISTP preferences are, however, less often attracted to careers and occupations in health-care practice, personal care and services, religious professions, arts/design/entertainment, sales, community and social services, and counseling/psychotherapy. They are typically found less often in careers that require a great deal of nurturing or relationship-oriented work, and work that requires attention to material that is highly theoretical or less tangible.

ISTPs who find themselves in—or drawn to—a career in which their type seems to be less frequent may want to read "Career Choices Where Your Type is Less Frequent" on page 24.

ISFP

Summary Career Description

ISFPs are most likely to find interesting and satisfying those careers that make use of their depth of concentration, their reliance on facts, their warmth and sympathy (i.e., their emphasis on interpersonal values), and their adaptability. ISFPs are very often found in careers that allow for direct practical care of people or hands-on detail work that may require much solitude. Their realistic grounding, depth of feeling, and very personal approach to life often draw them to careers where they can help others in very pragmatic ways. Though often hidden, their warm and sympathetic nature can be felt by others who know them, and they communicate kindness in ways that make them exceptional candidates for working with people in need, children, or animals.

Overall Style

In addition, ISFPs often have a special sympathy for things natural and they may feel quite comfortable working outdoors. Their ongoing enjoyment of the present moment and their tendency to express through action rather than words often lead to the development of a craftsmanlike elegance in whatever work they have chosen. ISFPs are quietly adaptable in their work, and they tend to be the most comfortable in jobs that not only take advantage of their keen attention to detail and sense of aesthetics, but which also allow them a fair degree of freedom from restricting structures and rules. Their idealism and deep feeling make them particularly sensitive to the suffering of others, which leads to their wanting to help others in very practical ways.

Appealing Environments, Tasks, Roles

ISFPs are often found in environments or roles where detailed knowledge may be required and where they can express their caring and concern for others in direct or indirect ways. They are also drawn to tasks and arenas where they can deal with facts rather than theory, where they feel their work contributes to something that they care about, where they can work with people in generally noncompetitive situations, and where they can make use of practical action skills. ISFPs report being attracted to career environments that are interpersonally supportive and that foster a degree of harmony, and where they can work independently to some degree, but where they can still be involved with others. ISFPs enjoy working with others, but are not particularly inclined to want to manage, supervise, or lead groups of people, although they can and will decidedly do so if their inner ideals require it of them.

Job Search Style

For ISFPs the job search tends to be a practical and people-oriented process. They are excellent gatherers of information, and their warm and personal orientation can open doors for gathering information from people they know and trust. Their pragmatic people orientation, hands-on abilities, and adaptability will usually be communicated to others during the job search. Potential drawbacks for ISFPs in the job search include a tendency to overlook unusual job opportunities or options, an unwillingness to look at the long-term consequences of a job decision, and a tendency to undervalue their accomplishments. Under stress, ISFPs can become quite critical of others and feel incompetent as they engage in the job-search process. If they notice this trend, they can benefit from attending to the more empowering facts of the situation, which may include acknowledging their skills and the importance of communicating them to others. They may also benefit from moderating their idealism and expectations about jobs and the job search.

Career Areas: More Attractive

People with ISFP preferences are often attracted to careers and occupations in the following areas:

- Veterinary medicine
- Nursing
- Applied engineering specialties and engineering technician
- Medical technology
- Surveying and gardening
- Office and administrative support
- Personal care and services
- Computer operations and data analysis
- Physical therapy
- Bookkeeping
- Medicine: obstetrics, gynecology, pediatrics, family practice
- Transportation
- Aviation: air crew
- Recreation and coaching
- Health education
- Religious education
- Teaching: K–12
- Storekeeper
- Law enforcement: detective
- Construction
- Crafts and trades: carpenter, electrician, other trades

But ISFPs can find satisfaction and success in entirely different areas than those listed here. The key to *getting where one wants to go* involves first identifying what one *really* wants—something that comes from a more individual place than type. Individuals with ISFP preferences then need to use knowledge of their type to gain insight into how they might approach the different activities involved in planning a career. In other words, ISFPs need to build on the strengths of their type and address potential obstacles that may come along with their style as they explore options, connect with others, make decisions, and manage their careers.

Career Areas: Less Attractive

Every type is in virtually every career, and clearly people are drawn to careers for many reasons other than their type. People with ISFP preferences are, however, less often attracted to careers and occupations that require a great deal of impersonal analysis of nontangible, symbolic, and technical material, such as in the physical and life sciences, systems analysis and finance. In addition, they are less drawn to highly organized and structured careers that require tough-minded approaches to people or things, such as in management, administration, and law. ISFPs are also found less often in the performing and fine arts and in media and entertainment.

ISFPs who find themselves in—or drawn to—a career in which their type seems to be less frequent may want to read "Career Choices Where Your Type is Less Frequent" on page 24.

INFP
Introverted Feeling with Extraverted Intuition

Summary Career Description

INFPs are most likely to find interesting and satisfying those careers that make use of their depth of concentration, their grasp of possibilities, their warmth and sympathy (i.e., their emphasis on interpersonal values), and their adaptability. INFPs are very often found in careers where there are opportunities for creating something new, communicating about ideas, or where there are opportunities to help others. Their very personal approach to life, their sensitivity to people, and their willingness to look beyond what is present and obvious often draw them to careers in which they can foster growth and development in others. They are also drawn to careers where they can communicate their ideas and insights—whether verbally or in writing.

Overall Style

Their idealism provides them with a strong sense of what constitutes the "good," especially where people are concerned. This idealism, in conjunction with their open-mindedness and tolerance, makes INFPs exceptionally well-suited to work in which a vision or understanding of human nature and potential is needed. At times, though, their perfectionism can hinder their work. Human values and concern for human issues are deeply important to INFPs; their deep feeling and warmth may not, however, be apparent at first meeting. What is more likely to be seen by others on meeting them is their adaptability, their focus on possibilities and their communication skills. They may have well-developed writing or speaking skills, are often drawn to higher education, and may have a particular affinity for languages and the arts. INFPs tend to dislike a great deal of structure or rules in their work, and they are usually patient with complexity.

Appealing Environments, Tasks, Roles

INFPs are often found in environments or roles where the work requires quiet concentration, where they can work with people in a more private, one-to-one relationship, and/or where interpersonal sensitivity is important. They are also drawn to tasks and arenas where they can be creative or where the work they do leads to an increased understanding of the human condition and ways human suffering can be alleviated. INFPs report being attracted to career environments where they can work with and develop relationships with others, particularly other creative and caring people, where they can help others, and where they feel the job has meaning and purpose. They also report being attracted to careers that allow them the flexibility to be creative, where they are intellectually stimulated, and where there is room for variety and learning. A degree of privacy and alone time in their work is usually very important to INFPs.

Job Search Style

For INFPs the job search can be an opportunity to use their creativity, flexibility, and skills in self-expression. They can generate a variety of job possibilities, consider them as an avenue to fulfill their values, and pursue them using their skills in communicating with others, either in writing or in person. Their idealism, commitment, responsiveness, and people skills will usually be communicated to others in the job search. Potential drawbacks for INFPs in the job search include unrealistic expectations for a job, feelings of inadequacy or lack of confidence, and inattention to the details of jobs or of the job search. Under stress, INFPs may become quite critical of others and themselves, and they may hold themselves back because they feel incompetent as they engage in this process. They can benefit from allowing their intuition to give them a new perspective on the possibilities available in the situation. They may also find it helpful to truly acknowledge their skills, as well as the importance of communicating those skills to others. In addition, INFPs can benefit from developing realistic expectations about the job search, and from objectively looking at the logical consequences of the various decisions they make, acknowledging their skills and the importance of communicating them to others. They may also benefit from moderating their idealism and expectations about jobs and the job search.

Career Areas: More Attractive

People with INFP preferences are often attracted to careers and occupations in the following areas:

- Fine artist
- Interior design
- Visual arts, graphic design, multimedia, animation
- Psychologist: clinical, counseling, educational
- Counseling, social work, community services
- Medicine: psychiatry
- Architecture
- Writing, editing
- Journalism and publishing
- Religious professions
- Social sciences
- Research
- Educational consulting
- Personal care and services
- Physical therapy
- Teaching: art, drama, music, English, languages
- Acting, performing arts and entertainment
- Musician, singer, composer
- Social and life sciences
- Public health careers

But INFPs can find satisfaction and success in entirely different areas than those listed here. The key to *getting where one wants to go* involves first identifying what one *really* wants—something that comes from a more individual place than type. Individuals with INFP preferences then need to use knowledge of their type to gain insight into how they might approach the different activities involved in planning a career. In other words, INFPs need to build on the strengths of their type and address potential obstacles that may come along with their style as they explore options, connect with others, make decisions, and manage their careers.

Career Areas: Less Attractive

Every type is in virtually every career, and clearly people are drawn to careers for many reasons other than their type. People with INFP preferences are, however, less often attracted to careers and occupations in management, business, the military, factory work, and other fields requiring attention to detail, systematic tough-minded analysis, or highly structured work. They are also found much less often in careers that require a great deal of interpersonal competition, or careers that involve a significant amount of hands-on, manual, or mechanical work, such as protective services, construction, and engineering.

INFPs who find themselves in—or drawn to—a career in which their type seems to be less frequent may want to read "Career Choices Where Your Type is Less Frequent" on page 24.

Summary Career Description

INTPs are most likely to find interesting and satisfying those careers that make use of their depth of concentration, their grasp of possibilities, their use of logic and analysis, and their adaptability. INTPs are very often found in academic, theoretical, and technical positions, many of which require prolonged periods of solitary concentration and tough-minded analysis. Their concern with ideas and their natural curiosity about the underlying principles and explanations for events often draws them to careers where an in-depth understanding of some abstract subject is required. Their abilities to become absorbed in an idea, to concentrate to the exclusion of all distractions, and to be objectively critical and creative often lead to their gaining a remarkable understanding of some complex problem, issue, or subject matter.

Overall Style

INTPs are drawn to careers in which problem analysis and creative solutions are required, and they may have exceptional skills in finding inconsistencies, critiquing a situation, and offering remedies. These skills apply to whatever field they have chosen, whether it is computer programming, market analysis, science, writing, editing, or law. INTPs are also often found in settings where ideas and inspiration are primary; hence they are often drawn to the academic setting, both as students and teachers. They enjoy being around those who share their own drive to understand, and as teachers, they are more inclined to work with advanced students. INTPs often have strong needs for freedom, autonomy, and variety, and what is often first observed in them is their easy adaptability and creative lifestyle. INTPs tend to resist a great deal of structure and rules in their work, and they need private time for the introspective analysis that is their hallmark.

Appealing Environments, Tasks, Roles

INTPs are often found in environments or roles where theory development is important, where the manipulation of abstract ideas or information is necessary, and that require a more objective or analytic approach to people or things. They are also drawn to tasks and arenas where there is a stream of new problems or situations to challenge them; careers that allow for time alone, thinking, and imagining; and careers that allow for more independence and creativity. INTPs report being attracted to career environments where they can focus attention on the problem-solving process rather than on end products or the realistic application of their ideas. They are less inclined to supervise or organize others, and if they do work with others, they prefer working with persons they see as skilled and competent.

Job Search Style

For INTPs the job search is an opportunity to use their analytical skills, their creativity, and their adaptability. They can conceive of a variety of job opportunities, see the long-term consequences of decisions, and be innovative both in the job search and in marketing their skills. Their critical thinking ability, ingenuity, and flexibility will usually be communicated to others in the job search. Potential drawbacks for INTPs in the job search include unrealistic expectations for a job or the job search, inaction, failure to establish rapport with others or to attend to the interpersonal requirements of the job search, and reluctance to make a decision. Under stress, INTPs can feel overwhelmed as they engage in this process and can benefit from allowing their insight to provide them with new ideas or perspectives on the situation. They may also find it useful to determine what is important to them and to act and follow through on the important details of the job search. INTPS may also benefit from considering what is truly of value to them, which can provide the drive to persevere and follow through on all parts of the job search.

Career Areas: More Attractive

People with INTP preferences are often attracted to careers and occupations in the following areas:

- Computing and systems administration
- Architecture
- Fine arts
- Graphic design
- Life and physical sciences: biology, chemistry, geology
- Social sciences
- Political science
- Information sciences
- Research
- Law: attorney, judge
- Journalism
- Writing and editing
- Executive: law, computing, construction
- Photography
- Psychology: industrial, organizational, other
- Acting, entertainment, directing, and producing
- Pharmacy
- Engineering: biomedical, software, aerospace, civil, other
- Medicine: pathology, psychiatry, other
- Teaching: university
- Electronics

But INTPs can find satisfaction and success in entirely different areas than those listed here. The key to *getting where one wants to go* involves first identifying what one *really* wants—something that comes from a more individual place than type. Individuals with INTP preferences then need to use knowledge of their type to gain insight into how they might approach the different activities involved in planning a career. In other words, INTPs need to build on the strengths of their type and address potential obstacles that may come along with their style as they explore options, connect with others, make decisions, and manage their careers.

Career Areas: Less Attractive

Every type is in virtually every career, and clearly people are drawn to careers for many reasons other than their type. People with INTP preferences are, however, less often attracted to careers and occupations that involve a great deal of direct human service work or that require ongoing attention to people's emotional lives or daily needs, including for example the religious professions, nursing, personal services, or teaching young people. They are also found less often in careers that involve highly structured or detail-oriented work, or require living in an environment that demands a great deal of routine, such as in military or corrections work.

INTPs who find themselves in—or drawn to—a career in which their type seems to be less frequent may want to read "Career Choices Where Your Type is Less Frequent" on page 24.

ESTP

Summary Career Description

ESTPs are most likely to find interesting and satisfying those careers that make use of their breadth of interests, their reliance on facts, their use of logic and analysis, and their adaptability. ESTPs are found in a variety of careers, but are most often found in careers that require an active, realistic, and hands-on approach. Their realistic grounding, adaptability, and desire for contact with the world often draw them to careers in trades, business and sales, law enforcement, and some of the technically oriented professions. They learn best from firsthand experience, and their active curiosity about the world in conjunction with their tough-minded and analytic approach to decision making, can make them superbly pragmatic problem solvers. They may also be skilled in dealing with interpersonal conflict and capable of convincing or negotiating well with others.

Overall Style

ESTPs are often found in careers that require an ongoing practical adaptation to changing circumstances; they can make excellent troubleshooters. Their analytical skills are used on the facts of a situation, and thus they may also be good at making use of available resources. At times ESTPs may not mind bending the rules to get something. In addition, they may demonstrate a remarkable memory for facts and details, which is related to their active willingness to be fully involved in life experiences, an involvement that can drive them to take great enjoyment in all things physical. Possible extensions of their approach to life include becoming very skilled in the use of certain tools or instruments and seeking out work where they can enjoy a degree of risk.

Appealing Environments, Tasks, Roles

ESTPs typically enjoy jobs that do not place too much structure or too many rules on them, and they usually need a great deal of contact with people. ESTPs are often found in environments or roles where they can troubleshoot, explore, experiment, and have a sense of freedom. They are also drawn to tasks and arenas where they can deal with specifics, work with things that can be seen, or promote something. ESTPs report being attracted to career environments that offer them change and variety and where they can have fun. They also often enjoy responding and adapting to unplanned situations. They are often drawn to public and protective service work, as well as personal service work.

Job Search Style

For ESTPs the job search is an extremely practical process. They can actively make connections with others and/or make use of past connections to gather information on jobs, they can critically and objectively look at the realities of what will be required in the job search, and they can typically sell themselves well. Their energy, adaptability, and practicality are usually communicated to others during the job search. Potential drawbacks for ESTPs in the job search include a tendency to focus only on the immediate present rather than on long-term job plans, failure to consider unusual job opportunities or career paths, and failure to follow through or to communicate seriousness and dependability. Under stress, ESTPs may feel very confused or inappropriately see negative meanings in many events during the job search process. They may find it useful to engage their objectivity to analyze the realities of a situation, and they may benefit from understanding that their options are not really closed off if they develop long-range career plans.

Career Areas: More Attractive

People with ESTP preferences are often attracted to careers and occupations in the following areas:

- Marketing and sales
- Law enforcement: police officer and detective
- Construction and trades: carpentry, other
- Protective services: firefighter, other
- Aviation and transportation: pilot, air crew, driver
- Military careers
- Forestry, gardening, farming, fishing
- Banking
- Credit investigator and loan officer
- Recreation
- Business and finance
- Tax examiner and auditor
- Engineering: materials, other
- Reporter and editor
- Machinist and mechanic
- Electrical or electronic installation and repair
- Pharmacy
- Real estate and insurance sales
- Business management
- Bartending, chef and cook
- Management and supervision: military, agriculture, trades

But ESTPs can find satisfaction and success in entirely different areas than those listed here. The key to *getting where one wants to go* involves first identifying what one *really* wants—something that comes from a more individual place than type. Individuals with ESTP preferences then need to use knowledge of their type to gain insight into how they might approach the different activities involved in planning a career. In other words, ESTPs need to build on the strengths of their type and address potential obstacles that may come along with their style as they explore options, connect with others, make decisions, and manage their careers.

Career Areas: Less Attractive

Every type is in virtually every career, and clearly people are drawn to careers for many reasons other than their type. People with ESTP preferences are, however, less often attracted to careers and occupations that require interests or skills in the theoretical, abstract, or symbolic, such as in architecture, life, physical and social sciences, and careers in the arts or teaching. They also tend to be found much less often in organized human care roles such as psychology, health care, and the religious professions.

ESTPs who find themselves in—or drawn to—a career in which their type seems to be less frequent may want to read "Career Choices Where Your Type is Less Frequent" on page 24.

ESFP

Summary Career Description

ESFPs are most likely to find interesting and satisfying those careers that make use of their breadth of interests, their reliance on facts, their warmth and sympathy (i.e., their emphasis on interpersonal values), and their adaptability. ESFPs are found in a variety of careers, many of which include active health and human services, such as nursing, teaching, and child care. Their warmth, enthusiasm, attention to detail, and realistic grounding often draw them to these people-oriented careers, as well as business and office careers. They learn best from firsthand experience, and their active curiosity about the world often leads them to seek ongoing involvement not only with people, but also in all things physical, which often draws them to active outside jobs as well.

Overall Style

Their realistic acceptance of the facts, their open-minded tolerance, and their tactful, sympathetic approach to others can make them exceptionally skilled in any career that requires them to meet, work with, or entertain people. They thoroughly enjoy being with others and may also be quite skilled in remembering facts about the people with whom they work. ESFPs value cooperation and may also have skills in managing conflicts. Their trust of the facts and their ability to respond to the needs of the moment often translate into pragmatic problem-solving skills: they can make excellent troubleshooters. Realists at heart, they may be comfortable bending the rules to make things work. They may also have a flair for the aesthetic and can be skilled at jobs that involve designing, molding, or shaping, particularly when the work is hands-on and uses tangible materials. ESFPs typically like jobs that allow them freedom to be active and where there is less structure.

Appealing Environments, Tasks, Roles

ESFPs are often found in environments or roles where ongoing and practical contact with people is required, where hands-on work is involved, or where some detailed practical knowledge is necessary. They are inclined to put more trust in, and learn better from, firsthand experience. They are also drawn to tasks and arenas that allow them to be actively involved with a variety of people, where they can serve, help, or guide others; and where there is a great deal of flexibility and room for spontaneity. ESFPs report being attracted to career environments where there is some excitement in the work, and they often say it is important for a job to be fun. ESFPs like to be personally involved in their work and to be where the action is; they are often naturals for being in or working with groups.

Job Search Style

For ESFPs the job search is a pragmatic process and an extension of their very personal style. They can make use of past connections with people or establish new connections easily to gather job information, and they are often excellent at selling themselves and their adaptability. Their pragmatic people orientation and people skills, their flexibility, and their command of the facts are usually communicated to others during the job search. Potential drawbacks for ESFPs in the job search include a tendency to overlook unusual job options, lack of planning and concern with the long view in their job search, and a tendency to put off decision making. Under stress, ESFPs may feel very confused or inappropriately see negative meanings in many events during the job search process. They may find it useful to engage their feeling to decide what is important to them, and they may benefit from understanding that their options are not really closed off if they develop long-range career plans.

Career Areas: More Attractive

People with ESFP preferences are often attracted to careers and occupations in the following areas:

- Health care and health-care support
- Medical technology
- Respiratory therapy
- Hospitality and lodging
- Fitness and training
- Sales
- Social services
- Counseling
- Veterinary medicine
- Child care
- Recreation, coaching, and lifeguard
- Religious education
- Nursing
- Construction and trades
- Transportation
- Pharmacy
- Designer
- Cosmetology
- Library worker
- Outdoor careers: gardening, forestry, farming, fishing
- Office administration, support, bookkeeping

But ESFPs can find satisfaction and success in entirely different areas than those listed here. The key to *getting where one wants to go* involves first identifying what one *really* wants—something that comes from a more individual place than type. Individuals with ESFP preferences then need to use knowledge of their type to gain insight into how they might approach the different activities involved in planning a career. In other words, ESFPs need to build on the strengths of their type and address potential obstacles that may come along with their style as they explore options, connect with others, make decisions, and manage their careers.

Career Areas: Less Attractive

Every type is in virtually every career, and clearly people are drawn to careers for many reasons other than their type. People with ESFP preferences are, however, less often attracted to careers and occupations that are highly structured, oriented largely to theory and technology, or are largely quantitative, such as careers in engineering, management, finance and computer sciences. They also tend to be found much less often in careers that require a more impersonal and analytical approach to people, as in the social sciences or law, or that have very little contact with people, as in research.

ESFPs who find themselves in—or drawn to—a career in which their type seems to be less frequent may want to read "Career Choices Where Your Type is Less Frequent" on page 24.

ENFP
Extraverted Intuition with Introverted Feeling

Summary Career Description

ENFPs are most likely to find interesting and satisfying those careers that make use of their breadth of interests, their grasp of possibilities, their warmth and sympathy (i.e., their emphasis on interpersonal values), and their adaptability. ENFPs are often found in careers where they can be creative; and work with people, understand them, and foster their growth. Their interest in symbols, meaning, and human relationships also attracts them to careers that require communication and expression, whether in oral or written form. They want to pursue new horizons, and in working with others this often shows as a desire to draw out the possibilities in those people. Whatever field they choose, their imagination and enthusiasm lead them to want to be innovative, and they are drawn to think of, as well as initiate new projects and new ways of doing things.

Overall Style

Their spontaneity, warmth, optimism, and keen interpersonal perceptions can make them exceptionally skillful in working with people, whether they have chosen to encounter others through sales, teaching, counseling, or any other people-oriented career. ENFPs may be remarkably skilled at motivating others, and usually feel at home working with groups of people. Their adaptability allows them to work with others, or in any career setting, from inspiration rather than from a plan, and they typically prefer to have relatively few rules or structures in their work environment. ENFPs can often develop skills in any field that truly interests them. Their facility with symbols and their interest in meaning and the abstract often lead them to the arts as a mode of self-expression, but their skills and interests may lead them into the sciences as well.

Appealing Environments, Tasks, Roles

ENFPs are often found in environments or roles where they can follow their inspirations to initiate a variety of new activities, and finding solutions to problems energizes them. They do not sit still for long due to their active involvement with the world. They are also drawn to environments where there are opportunities to be creative, such as careers in the expressive or fine arts. ENFPs report being attracted to careers that allow for challenge and variety, and where they can work with ideas and continue to learn. They want work that they can care about, where they can work with and help people, and where self-expression and creativity are possible. They would also rather be involved in the beginning or start-up phases of a project than be responsible for detail work and follow-through.

Job Search Style

For ENFPs the job search can be an opportunity to use their energy, creativity, and adaptability. They can imagine a variety of job possibilities, make use of their wide variety of relationships to gather information about job opportunities and market themselves with confidence. Their ingenuity, enthusiasm, and people skills will usually be communicated to others during the job search. Potential draw-backs for the ENFP in the job search include unrealistic expectations about jobs or the job search, a tendency to let opportunities pass by for lack of decision making, and failure to be organized or to follow through on important details. Under stress, ENFPs may become withdrawn and listless, or they may become inappropriately concerned with the details of the job search. They may find it helpful to reconsider what their values are and what is important to them as they attend to the realities of the job search, and to appreciate the necessity of taking a measured approach to the job search process.

Career Areas: More Attractive

People with ENFP preferences are often attracted to careers and occupations in the following areas:

- Entertainment: acting, directing
- Fine arts and visual arts
- Music and composing
- Psychology: clinical, counseling, educational
- Counseling and social work
- Hospitality and lodging
- Journalism and writing
- Religious professions and education
- Social sciences
- Health care and health-care support
- Teaching: arts, adult education, preschool, kindergarten
- Cosmetology
- Sales
- Public relations
- Computing
- Photography
- Education: administration, consulting
- Recreation: trainer
- Forestry
- Landscape architecture
- Child care

But ENFPs can find satisfaction and success in entirely different areas than those listed here. The key to *getting where one wants to go* involves first identifying what one *really* wants—something that comes from a more individual place than type. Individuals with ENFP preferences then need to use knowledge of their type to gain insight into how they might approach the different activities involved in planning a career. In other words, ENFPs need to build on the strengths of their type and address potential obstacles that may come along with their style as they explore options, connect with others, make decisions, and manage their careers.

Career Areas: Less Attractive

Every type is in virtually every career, and clearly people are drawn to careers for many reasons other than their type. People with ENFP preferences are, however, less often attracted to careers and occupations that require a great deal of precision and logical analysis, or careers that are highly structured, such as careers in management, the military, or engineering. They are also found less often in careers that require work in isolation or careers that demand a great deal of routine hands-on, manual or mechanical work, as in production or repair jobs.

ENFPs who find themselves in—or drawn to—a career in which their type seems to be less frequent may want to read "Career Choices Where Your Type is Less Frequent" on page 24.

ENTP

Summary Career Description

ENTPs are most likely to find interesting and satisfying those careers that make use of their breadth of interests, their grasp of possibilities, their use of logic and analysis, and their adaptability. ENTPs are found in a variety of diverse careers, but the fields in which they work typically allow them to engage their inventive and analytical minds. Their creativity, comfort with the abstract, and problem-solving abilities often attract them to careers in the fields of science, communications, and technology. Because they are stimulated by complexity and new problems to solve, they are often found in careers where there is a stream of new challenges and/or where troubleshooting plays a part. Whatever fields they choose, their energy and desire for innovation lead them to think of, as well as initiate new projects and envision new ways of doing things.

Overall Style

Competence is usually of great importance to ENTPs, and they may enjoy careers where they can continually test out their abilities to analyze, debate, convince, improvise, and succeed. ENTPs can often develop skills in any field that truly interests them. They usually have a great deal of enthusiasm and confidence not only in their ideas but also in their ability to succeed, which often translates into skill in influencing or winning the support of others. They tend to be nonconformists, and their sureness in the value of their insights can serve to justify their willingness to go around the system; they may have an entrepreneurial character. ENTPs value autonomy and excitement, and usually resist having too many rules or too much structure in their work. Due to the energy of their ideas and inspirations, ENTPs are not inclined to sit still for long.

Appealing Environments, Tasks, Roles

ENTPs are often found in environments or roles where they can be independent and feel competent; where there is the opportunity for variety, creativity, and innovation; and where ideas are important. They are also drawn to tasks and arenas where creativity and expression in the external world are important, as in careers in the arts. ENTPs report being attracted to career environments where they can interact with many different people and where they can be action oriented. They also prefer to leave details and follow-up to others. Their outgoingness, more analytic stance, and keen perceptions of other people can make them successful in careers that require more objective approaches to people, as in law, public relations, or marketing.

Job Search Style

For ENTPs the job search can be an opportunity to use their energy, creativity, and flexibility. They can usually imagine a wide range of possibilities, analyze what needs to be done to maximize their chances in the job search, and enthusiastically market themselves. Their enthusiasm, ingenuity, and thoughtful adaptability will usually be communicated to others in the job search. Potential drawbacks for ENTPs in the job search include inattention to the facts and details of jobs or of the job search, inattention to the emotional climate of interviews, and a tendency to allow opportunities to pass by due to lack of decision making or follow-through activities. Under stress, they may become withdrawn and listless, or they may become inappropriately concerned with the details of the job search. They may find it helpful to objectively analyze the realities of their situation and to understand the necessity of taking a measured approach to the job search process.

Career Areas: More Attractive

People with ENTP preferences are often attracted to careers and occupations in the following areas:

- Arts and entertainment
- Manager and executive: arts, entertainment, media
- Journalism, visual arts, photography
- Acting
- Life and physical sciences: geology, biology, chemistry, economics
- Social sciences
- Marketing and public relations
- Finance
- Executive: business, finance, health care
- Human resources
- Computing: analyst, programmer, administrator
- Management consulting
- Sales and advertising
- Manager and executive: sales, education, training
- Psychology: industrial/organizational
- Engineering: industrial, aeronautical, electrical, chemical
- Architecture
- Executive: architecture, engineering, transportation, production
- Computer and electrical technician
- Law
- Construction and skilled trades

But ENTPs can find satisfaction and success in entirely different areas than those listed here. The key to *getting where one wants to go* involves first identifying what one *really* wants—something that comes from a more individual place than type. Individuals with ENTP preferences then need to use knowledge of their type to gain insight into how they might approach the different activities involved in planning a career. In other words, ENTPs need to build on the strengths of their type and address potential obstacles that may come along with their style as they explore options, connect with others, make decisions, and manage their careers.

Career Areas: Less Attractive

Every type is in virtually every career, and clearly people are drawn to careers for many reasons other than their type. People with ENTP preferences are, however, less often attracted to careers and occupations that require a great deal of pragmatic personal care or the fostering of relationships, as in careers in child care, teaching younger students (preschool through grade 12), nursing, health-care support, or religious careers. They are also found less often in careers that require work in isolation or careers that demand a great deal of routine hands-on or mechanical work, as in office support, production, or repair jobs.

ENTPs who find themselves in—or drawn to—a career in which their type seems to be less frequent may want to read "Career Choices Where Your Type is Less Frequent" on page 24.

ESTJ

Summary Career Description

ESTJs are most likely to find interesting and satisfying those careers that make use of their breadth of interests, their reliance on facts, their use of logic and analysis, and their ability to organize. ESTJs are often found in careers that require the use of tough-minded, fact-oriented, and goal-directed analysis to actively organize, build structure, and give direction. They are found in high numbers in management and administrative positions. Their energetic orientation to action, along with their pragmatic and realistic decision-making style, often attracts them to these roles. They are usually comfortable applying their standards of what is correct, efficient, and sensible to all aspects of their environment, and thus they can be very analytical and matter-of-fact in their evaluations not only of situations, but of people as well.

Overall Style

Their systematic approach to getting the job done and their ongoing respect for details and rules often communicate a sense of responsibility and sturdy reliability to others who feel they can be trusted to follow work through to completion. Decision making usually comes naturally to them, but they want their decisions to be based on hard facts, and they are typically more interested in organizing what is going on at the moment rather than in organizing abstract systems. ESTJs are often drawn to the useful applications of the field in which they find themselves, and thus they tend to be found in careers in which pragmatic and tangible results can be seen. They are often found in business and industry, but they demonstrate a willingness to organize and a pragmatic task-orientation regardless of the chosen area of work.

Appealing Environments, Tasks, Roles

ESTJs are often found in environments or roles that require an objective approach to people and that involve hands-on work. Opportunities to interact with others are important to ESTJs, as are work environments that are structured and which have relatively clear lines of procedure. They are also drawn to tasks and arenas where they can work systematically, and they like working on concrete and straightforward projects where there are clear outcomes and objective standards. ESTJs report being attracted to career environments where they can manage organizations, provide leadership, be involved in practical applications of concepts to real-world problems, and achieve some success and stability. They like feeling productive and enjoy working with others who are also conscientious and production oriented.

Job Search Style

For ESTJs the job search is a very pragmatic process and a natural extension of their approach to the world. Decision making tends to come naturally to them, and they are efficient and thorough in their gathering of information and in their marketing of themselves. Their ability to network, their stability, and their logical and realistic approach to work are usually communicated to others during the job search. Potential drawbacks for ESTJs in the job search may include failure to consider unusual opportunities, making decisions too quickly, and a tendency to be unaware of the interpersonal climate of interviews. Under stress, they may feel overwhelmed or become oversensitive to perceived criticisms of their competence as they engage in the job search. They may find it useful to take another look at the facts and realities of their situation, and to consider the importance of staying open to possibilities and to the roles relationships play in the job search process.

Career Areas: More Attractive

People with ESTJ preferences are often attracted to careers and occupations in the following areas:

- Protective services: law enforcement, firefighting, corrections

- Management: general

- Management and supervision: mechanics, agriculture, construction

- Management and supervision: protective services

- Production and manufacturing: technician, operations, supervision

- Accounting

- Banking and finance

- Purchasing

- Administration: education, health care

- Construction and trades

- Teaching: trades and technical

- Executive and manager: transportation, building, grounds

- Sales and sales management

- Insurance broker and real estate

- Executive and manager: architecture, engineering

- Management consulting

- Military

- Engineering: civil, mechanical, chemical

- Aviation: pilot

- Law: judge

But ESTJs can find satisfaction and success in entirely different areas than those listed here. The key to *getting where one wants to go* involves first identifying what one *really* wants—something that comes from a more individual place than type. Individuals with ESTJ preferences then need to use knowledge of their type to gain insight into how they might approach the different activities involved in planning a career. In other words, ESTJs need to build on the strengths of their type and address potential obstacles that may come along with their style as they explore options, connect with others, make decisions, and manage their careers.

Career Areas: Less Attractive

Every type is in virtually every career, and clearly people are drawn to careers for many reasons other than their type. People with ESTJ preferences are, however, less often attracted to careers and occupations that require a great deal of human service work or that require emotional care of others, such as careers in counseling, health-care support, child care, social services, or the religious professions. In addition they are found less often in work that requires ongoing attention to more theoretical, abstract, or symbolic material, such as careers in the arts or fine arts, journalism, or the social sciences, or teaching in these fields.

ESTJs who find themselves in—or drawn to—a career in which their type seems to be less frequent may want to read "Career Choices Where Your Type is Less Frequent" on page 24.

ESFJ

Summary Career Description

ESFJs are most likely to find interesting and satisfying those careers that make use of their breadth of interests, their reliance on facts, their warmth and sympathy (i.e., their emphasis on interpersonal values), and their ability to organize. ESFJs are often found in careers characterized by a great deal of communication, nurturance and people-oriented work, including teaching and spiritually oriented roles. Their energy, warmth, and compassion attracts them to any field in which they can find practical ways of working with and helping others, and they are often skilled in promoting and supporting fellowship and harmony. They have a well developed sense of duty and will work hard to get the job done. Their idealism and concern for tradition and community can lead to a strong sense of connectedness and loyalty to an organization that shares their values and to people with whom they work.

Overall Style

ESFJs tend to be orderly and attentive to detail, particularly when the details are in support of their people values, and thus they are often found in careers in which they can be both nurturing and conscientious, such as teaching, health care, or personal services. ESFJs are interested in pragmatic and realistic activities, whether they are helping others or are otherwise engaged, and they have less patience for the purely abstract or theoretical. Their ability to attend to the strengths of others, in conjunction with their outgoing nature, can be a positive influence on other people. As a result, they can be quite influential through their relationships, a skill that may be of use in whatever career area they choose, whether their interests are in sales, teaching, managing, or some other area. ESFJs usually want and need contact with others in their careers, appreciate a degree of structure in their work, and often adapt well to routine.

Appealing Environments, Tasks, Roles

ESFJs are often found in environments or roles that are people oriented; where they can nurture, care for, and help others grow; and where they can be active. They are also drawn to tasks and arenas where they can make use of their ability to attend to and manipulate facts and details, such as office or technical work. Duty is often a strong value for ESFJs, and they will exercise their organizing skills to ensure commitments are carried through, regardless of environment. They enjoy being productive, and report being attracted to career environments where they know that their work has practical benefits. ESFJs appreciate cooperative and harmonious work environments, but they also like exercising a degree of control and decision making in organizing their own work.

Job Search Style

For ESFJs the job search is a people-oriented and pragmatic process. They are able to develop networks and rely on existing relationships to aid in the gathering of information, as well as make use of organizational skills in preparing for and following through on the search. Their enthusiasm, warmth, and conscientiousness are usually communicated to others during the job search. Potential drawbacks for ESFJs in the job search may include a tendency to make decisions or evaluations of situations too quickly, ignoring objective or long-range considerations in career planning, a tendency to overlook unusual job possibilities or options, and sensitivity to rejection. Under stress, ESFJs may become excessively critical, not only of themselves, but also of others. They may also see career problems in a black-and-white manner and have unrealistic expectations for advice from experts. They can benefit from attending to all of the facts of their situation and from appreciating that harmony is not always necessary or possible in the job search.

Career Areas: More Attractive

People with ESFJ preferences are often attracted to careers and occupations in the following areas:

- Health-care support: physical therapy, pharmacy, radiology, veterinary
- Medical technology
- Lodging and hospitality
- Health care: dentist, pediatrics, family practice, surgery
- Management and supervision: health care, child care
- Nursing
- Management: office
- Religious professions
- Religious education
- Child care
- Office and administrative support
- Personal trainer
- Cosmetology
- Community and social services
- Teaching: preschool, kindergarten, elementary
- Teaching: vocational education
- Speech pathology
- Public health and health education
- Social service administration
- Educational administration: student personnel
- Landscaping and gardening

But ESFJs can find satisfaction and success in entirely different areas than those listed here. The key to *getting where one wants to go* involves first identifying what one *really* wants—something that comes from a more individual place than type. Individuals with ESFJ preferences then need to use knowledge of their type to gain insight into how they might approach the different activities involved in

planning a career. In other words, ESFJs need to build on the strengths of their type and address potential obstacles that may come along with their style as they explore options, connect with others, make decisions, and manage their careers.

Career Areas: Less Attractive

Every type is in virtually every career, and clearly people are drawn to careers for many reasons other than their type. People with ESFJ preferences are, however, less often attracted to careers and occupations that are characterized by a great deal of highly abstract, technical and tough-minded analytical work, as in computer sciences, engineering, economics, and physical sciences. They are also found much less often in careers where there may be low contact with people, where a more abstract, impersonal, or analytical approach to people is involved, or where pragmatic outcomes are not obvious, as in the social sciences, psychology, law, and careers in the arts.

ESFJs who find themselves in—or drawn to—a career in which their type seems to be less frequent may want to read "Career Choices Where Your Type is Less Frequent" on page 24.

ENFJ

Summary Career Description

ENFJs are most likely to find interesting and satisfying those careers that make use of their breadth of interests, their grasp of possibilities, their warmth and sympathy (i.e., their emphasis on interpersonal values), and their ability to organize. ENFJs are very often found in careers that require expressiveness, organization, imagination, and an interest in people's emotional, intellectual, and spiritual development. Their energy, warmth, and compassion suit them to work in any field in which they can work with and understand others, which, in conjunction with their focus on possibilities for people, often draws them to the religious professions, counseling, or teaching. Their enthusiasm, willingness to see the points of view of others, and tolerance of a variety of opinions often give them exceptional skills in working with groups and in promoting fellowship and harmony.

Overall Style

ENFJs are often excellent communicators; they may have a facility for languages, and may be natural public speakers. Energetic, creative, and naturally engaging, they can be quite persuasive and are often found in careers where they can and do influence others. They are often called on to be leaders. ENFJs can be charismatic and are also often found in the performing arts. They usually want and need contact with others in their careers, and they not only appreciate opportunities to help others develop, but also want opportunities to do so themselves. Decisive and organized, they appreciate structure, clear expectations, and enjoy being busy and productive; they often like juggling several projects at once.

Appealing Environments, Tasks, Roles

ENFJs are often found in environments or roles where they can establish relationships in a supportive environment, where they can help others grow and develop, and where they can work with groups. They tend to have a great curiosity for ideas, are comfortable with the abstract and symbolic, and are often drawn to tasks and arenas where creative or artistic expression form a part of the work. This is particularly true when the ideas and symbols can be used to make a difference for people. ENFJs report being attracted to career environments where there are opportunities to use their imagination, where they can feel challenged, where they can make their own decisions, and where they are recognized for their contributions. ENFJs report that they prefer to avoid work that requires too much attention to detail and factual accuracy.

Job Search Style

For ENFJs the job search is a natural extension of their energetic, people-oriented, and organized style. They are able to see a variety of job possibilities, develop a job search plan, and develop and rely on existing networks in gathering information and in marketing themselves. Their enthusiasm, their people and communication skills, and their creativity are usually communicated to others during the job search. Potential drawbacks for ENFJs in the job search may include a tendency to make decisions or evaluations of a situation too quickly, inattention to the details or facts of jobs or of the job search, and a tendency to take rejection personally. Under stress they may become excessively critical, not only of themselves, but of others. They may also see career problems in a black-and-white manner and have unrealistic expectations for advice from experts. They can benefit from allowing their intuition to provide a broader, more meaningful perspective on their situation, and from appreciating that harmony is not always necessary or possible in the job search.

Career Areas: More Attractive

People with ENFJ preferences are often attracted to careers and occupations in the following areas:

- Religious professions and religious education
- Counseling: mental health, school, career, crisis
- Community services and social work
- Fine arts and craft artist
- Arts and entertainment: actor, musician, composer
- Interior design
- Photography
- Teaching: art, drama, music, English, languages, vocational education
- Teaching: all levels
- Lodging and hospitality, and events and convention planning
- Medicine: family, general practice, psychiatry, other
- Writing and journalism
- Marketing, public relations, sales, and advertising
- Health education and home health care
- Psychology: clinical, counseling, educational, industrial, organizational
- Social and political sciences
- Optometry
- Dental hygiene
- Child care
- Management and administration: education, personal services
- Physical therapist

But ENFJs can find satisfaction and success in entirely different areas than those listed here. The key to *getting where one wants to go* involves first identifying what one *really* wants—something that comes from a more individual place than type. Individuals with ENFJ preferences then need to use knowledge of their type to gain insight into how they might approach the different activities involved in planning a career. In other words, ENFJs need to build on the strengths of their type and address potential obstacles that may come along with their style as they explore options, connect with others, make decisions, and manage their careers.

Career Areas: Less Attractive

Every type is in virtually every career, and clearly people are drawn to careers for many reasons other than their type. People with ENFJ preferences are, however, less often attracted to careers and occupations characterized by a great deal of technical or tough-minded analysis and attention to detail, as in engineering or computer operations. They are also found much less often in careers that involve a great deal of interpersonal conflict (as in police or corrections work), business management (particularly if that work is not related to a people-oriented or service profession), or careers that have a low level of contact with people and/or a significant amount of hands-on precision work, as in many out-of-doors jobs, production/construction, and repair and maintenance jobs.

ENFJs who find themselves in—or drawn to—a career in which their type seems to be less frequent may want to read "Career Choices Where Your Type is Less Frequent" on page 24.

ENTJ

Summary Career Description

ENTJs are most likely to find interesting and satisfying those careers that make use of their breadth of interests, their grasp of possibilities, their use of logic and analysis, and their ability to organize. ENTJs are very often found in careers that require drive, giving direction to others, innovation, and tough-minded analysis; hence, they are often found in management and leadership positions. Their active, energetic, and impersonal style of decision making; their strategic approach; and their need to make things happen often attracts them to positions where they can clarify a vision, work with competent people, and manage resources to systematically achieve goals. They are usually comfortable applying their clear sense of what is correct, efficient, and effective to all aspects of their environment, and thus they can be very analytical and matter-of-fact in their evaluations not only of situations, but of people as well.

Overall Style

Their orientation to action, the big picture, and future goals, in conjunction with their drive to establish structure and achieve, means they are often found in positions where they can make policy, plan for the future, and take on responsibility. ENTJs can be quite ambitious in their plans and goals, and they are often very aware of the uses of power in achieving goals. In general, opportunities to interact with others are important to ENTJs, and they value competence in other people as much as they value it in themselves. Logic rules for ENTJs, and they expect the world to make sense. This analytic stance, combined with their focus on symbols, theories, and the abstract often attracts them to careers in the sciences, particularly the physical sciences, though they are found in the social sciences as well. Whatever career area they have chosen, they are often oriented to problem solving, and they enjoy the challenge

of analyzing a complex issue and discovering a new and creative solution.

Appealing Environments, Tasks, Roles

ENTJs are often found in environments or roles where they can make use of their creativity, as well as their appreciation for ideas and complexity. They are found not only in technical positions but also in some arts-related careers as well. In addition, they are often drawn to tasks and arenas that are challenging and action oriented, where there are opportunities for leadership, where they can seek new solutions to problems, and where they can be self-determined. ENTJs report being attracted to career environments and roles where they can make decisions and get things to happen. In addition, they enjoy work where they can engage in long-range planning, where they can feel and demonstrate their competence, and where there are opportunities for advancement. They appreciate work environments that are structured and organized and that have logical and objective standards for evaluating performance and progress.

Job Search Style

For ENTJs the job search is an opportunity to use their analytic and planning skills, and their ability to approach the market in an organized and strategic fashion. Decision making comes naturally to them, and they are able to make use of networks to gather information and to achieve career search goals. Their drive, problem-solving abilities, competence, and willingness to take charge are usually communicated to others during the job search. Potential drawbacks for ENTJs in the job search may include making decisions too quickly and without enough information, a tendency to ignore the interpersonal climate of interviews, failure to communicate diplomacy in interactions with others, and impatience with the details of the job search. Under stress, they may feel overwhelmed or become oversensitive to perceived criticisms of their competence as they engage in the job search. They may then find it useful to consider alternative explanations to their initial belief about what is happening or why, or to understand that what is happening is not personal. They may also find it useful to consider the importance of patience and of staying open to the roles relationships play in the job search process.

Career Areas: More Attractive

People with ENTJ preferences are often attracted to careers and occupations in the following areas:

- Engineering: electrical, chemical, other
- Executive and manager: architecture, engineering
- Law: attorney, judge
- Executive and manager: legal
- Life, physical, and social sciences: biology, geology, chemistry, psychology
- Executive and manager: sciences, computers
- Business and finance
- Executive and manager: business, finance, operations
- Executive and manager: marketing, sales
- Human resources
- Marketing and sales
- Executive and manager: arts, entertainment, media
- Computing: analyst, systems administration
- Executive and manager: education, health, community services
- Urban planning
- Skilled trades and supervision of trade workers
- Production and manufacturing
- Management and educational consulting
- Teaching: university

- Psychology: industrial/organizational
- Medicine: anesthesiology, surgery, internal, research

But ENTJs can find satisfaction and success in entirely different areas than those listed here. The key to *getting where one wants to go* involves first identifying what one *really* wants—something that comes from a more individual place than type. Individuals with ENTJ preferences then need to use knowledge of their type to gain insight into how they might approach the different activities involved in planning a career. In other words, ENTJs need to build on the strengths of their type and address potential obstacles that may come along with their style as they explore options, connect with others, make decisions, and manage their careers.

Career Areas: Less Attractive

Every type is in virtually every career, and clearly people are drawn to careers for many reasons other than their type. People with ENTJ preferences are, however, less often attracted to careers and occupations that require ongoing attention to the spiritual, emotional, or personal needs of others, or that require high levels of pragmatic nurturance, including for example religious professions, nursing, healthcare support, or teaching young people. They are also found much less often in careers in the protective services and careers that require a fair amount of routine hands-on detail-oriented work, such as in building and grounds work and office and administrative support.

ENTJs who find themselves in—or drawn to—a career in which their type seems to be less frequent may want to read "Career Choices Where Your Type is Less Frequent" on page 24.

Looking at Next Steps

Gathering Information and Exploring Options

after reading your type description and reviewing any questionnaires you've taken (the ones in the first part of this book for example), you increased your ideas about career options.

- Are you seeking a first time career or job?
- Are you staying in your current career or organization?
- Do you want to modify your current role, get a different job in your same organization, or retool for a different career in the same organization?
- Do you need to adapt to your current role by learning new skills and behaviors?
- Are you considering a new career or job in a different organization?
- Is working for yourself an option?
- Do you need to get some of your needs met outside of your workplace?

People with different type preferences tend to use different methods to learn more about the careers and the options in which they are interested. Not surprisingly, different types tend to have different strengths and face different obstacles as they seek out more information on their career options.

Some of the different methods for learning more about your options include the following:

- Talking to professionals, such as counselors and coaches
- Talking to colleagues and other people, such as mentors and supervisors, people in the field you are exploring

- Connecting with professional organizations, such as those in your current field or the field in which you have interest
- Exploring online resources and databases, such as search engines and career resources
- Libraries and books, such as career resource libraries, trade publications, biographies, and other books

Which of these activities are *you* most inclined to use? You will want to start with activities that are consistent with your natural strengths. However, you will also want to gather career information using methods that may *not* be as natural for you to be sure you give yourself the best chance of finding out which career options may or may not fit for you.

Are you the Introvert who makes good use of quiet research and self-reflection, but who may miss important data because information interviews aren't your preferred way of learning about a career? Or are you the Extravert who feels very comfortable meeting with others for information interviews, but who may miss important data because you didn't log some individual research or self-reflection time?

The following lists describe activities often favored by or overlooked by the different types. Take a moment to note which activities you are likely to use (draw on those natural inclinations *first*) and also note which activities you might tend to ignore. Challenge yourself to try out these less familiar activities—you'll probably learn some new and different things about the career options you're considering.

If you are an EXTRAVERT . . .

Build on your tendency to . . .

- Network naturally—you may already have access to a large network
- Be comfortable with information interviewing

And also be aware that you . . .

- May discuss career options *too* much with others, and not do enough self-assessment and internal exploration
- May interact for the sake of interacting and not gather appropriate information

If you are an INTROVERT . . .

Build on your tendency to . . .

- Be comfortable taking time for reading and self-assessment
- Focus well and in-depth on career ideas you've developed based on self-reflection

And also be aware that you . . .

- May not explore, take advantage of, or enjoy networking activities or information interviews
- May isolate yourself and not seek input from others

If you are a SENSING type . . .

Build on your tendency to . . .

- Gather factual, concrete, and specific information about careers options (e.g., job availability, salaries, locations, training required)
- Make good use of a detailed career plan and to be thorough and efficient in follow-up
- Seek hands-on experiences such as interning or volunteering (especially ESs).
- Realistically assess the job market and your fit with various jobs

And also be aware that you . . .

- May have difficulty seeing alternatives when feeling stuck
- May not want to try something new or consider a career change
- May focus too much on past experience as the sole predictor of future options
- May not trust an exciting "hunch"

If you are an INTUITIVE type . . .

Build on your tendency to . . .

- Look for patterns and meaning in the information and assessments you have
- View your career plans and goals from a long-term perspective
- See alternatives to traditional career search and development paths and brainstorm creative ways of finding information
- See or create job opportunities that others may overlook

And also be aware that you . . .

- May have difficulty focusing or acting on just one or two of the vast number of possibilities
- May miss information available through actually trying something out
- May miss important factual material in your exploration or underestimate pragmatic steps in realizing a career option
- May not realistically assess the job market and/or your fit with certain jobs

EXPLORING OPTIONS. *In the spaces provided, write which methods of exploring options and gathering information you are most likely to use. Note also which methods you might overlook, but which could offer you some new kinds of information. You might find it helpful to talk about the different methods with someone else.*

If you are a THINKING type . . .

Build on your tendency to . . .

- Approach the career search in a strategic manner—you may like to work through analyses of interests, skills, and other information
- Do good objective research on a career option or employer
- Use reference materials and job analyses of various occupations (especially Introverts)

And also be aware that you . . .

- May be so focused on the strategic value of a job that you don't consider whether or not you would really *like* the job
- May expect the career search to go more logically than real life usually does
- May miss information available from significant others or people you trust, or may not trust that you just care about something

If you are a FEELING type . . .

Build on your tendency to . . .

- Have a good knowledge of your values and what's important to you as motivators
- Make use of networks, relationships and information-gathering interviews (especially if you are an EF)
- Connect formally or informally with coaches or counselors for career concerns

And also be aware that you . . .

- May be too idealistic and forget to analyze both the positives and negatives of a job or career option
- May overlook information available in more objective forms (e.g., internet, career resource library)
- May be less willing to consider the long-term implications of a particular career option

If you are a JUDGING type . . .

Build on your tendency to . . .

- Organize career information and resources well, making efficient use of them
- Set goals, plan the tasks needed to reach those goals, and meet deadlines in achieving those goals

And also be aware that you . . .

- May become bored with information gathering and move to premature closure and thus define your career choice(s) too soon
- May not see new information that could lead to a better choice if that information seems inconsistent with your initial direction

If you are a PERCEIVING type . . .

Build on your tendency to . . .

- Be open to gathering and exploring new information and career options
- Adapt to a variety of possible careers

And also be aware that you . . .

- May continue to gather information when you really need to make decisions or a career choice
- May have difficulty committing to one course of action (even in the short run)

Evaluating Opportunities and Making Decisions

After you have gathered information about yourself and various careers, begin to evaluate your opportunities and make some decisions about what career or career options you are going to pursue further.

Here again, people with different type preferences tend to approach evaluating and deciding in different ways. People will differ in how they make these decisions including in the timing, amount of consideration of the options, and how much weight they will give the various options. The following method may help you evaluate your opportunities and make decisions in a more thorough and informed way.

Sensing, Intuition, Thinking, and Feeling all come into play in career decision making. The following Zig-Zag model can help you learn to make better use of all four of those processes. In using this model, you use your tools of perception (Sensing and Intuition) to see all aspects of your situation, and your tools of judgment (Thinking and Feeling) to make decisions based on both impersonal and personal criteria. The following chart shows you how.

Career development does not rest on one big decision, but rather involves a series of decisions. At this point, it is efficient to think about some part of the career exploration process about which you need more clarity. Keep that issue in mind as you go through the following steps of the Zig-Zag process. You may find it helpful to write down ideas or discuss them with someone else as you go through the four steps.

Step One: Sensing Perception

You use Sensing to determine the facts, data, and givens in a situation. You use Sensing to face the realities of whatever career issue is before you. Following are some questions that can help you use your Sensing perception.

- What is your job history?
- What work activities have been most satisfying/frustrating?
- How are things now?
- What is your MBTI type? What are your values, interests, skills? What education do you have?
- What jobs, roles, and salaries are currently available?

Step Two: Intuitive Perception

You use Intuition to look at the possibilities in a situation, and/or ways to change a situation. You use Intuition to notice meanings and patterns in the career information you have, and to put it in the context of your life and your future. Following are some questions that can help you use your Intuitive perception.

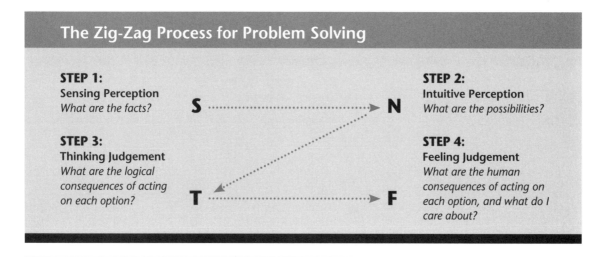

The Zig-Zag Process for Problem Solving

STEP 1:
Sensing Perception
What are the facts?

S

STEP 2:
Intuitive Perception
What are the possibilities?

N

STEP 3:
Thinking Judgement
What are the logical consequences of acting on each option?

T

STEP 4:
Feeling Judgement
What are the human consequences of acting on each option, and what do I care about?

F

- What do you become aware of as you open your mind to patterns in the information you have? Are there any patterns in the careers you consider or reject?

- What new or different possibilities come up when you brainstorm and set aside the belief that you are considering the one and only right thing?

- Are there options that keep coming to you that make no sense but are difficult to discount?

- What career or job options create the greatest long-term opportunity, offer a chance for growth, or fit with long-term plans?

- Are there less traveled or unusual ways to get to the career or job option I'm considering?

Step Three: Thinking Judgment

You use Thinking to make a critical and impersonal analysis of the situation: the career facts and career possibilities you discovered in the past two steps. You use Thinking to look at all of the consequences, both good and bad, of the various choices you have available to you. Following are some questions that can help you engage your Thinking judgment.

- If you step outside of yourself and the situation, what do you see objectively, impersonally, and critically?

- Based on your knowledge of yourself, how well or how poorly would you fit in the careers you are considering?

- What would be the positive and negative consequences of acting on each career possibility on your list? In other words, what are the logical outcomes of choosing each career?

- Are you able to be hard-headed about options that involve ideas or people you care about? It's important to be tough-minded in areas where you are least likely to be so.

Now that you have stepped outside yourself, it's time to reintroduce the personal element into the decision-making process.

Step Four: Feeling Judgment

You use Feeling to weigh how much you care about the possible outcomes of the different career options, and what each choice means to you personally. You use Feeling to give weight not only to your personal values, but also to the values and feelings of those about whom you care. Following are some questions that can help you engage your Feeling judgment.

- What do you care about in your life and career? What is important to you?

- As you look at your options, does a part of you quickly say: this is right or wrong; this is good or bad?

- If you acted on each possibility on your list, what would be the effect on you, on other people important in your life, and on your relationship with them?

- What careers do you really care about, even if you think it is illogical for them to seem so important? Take what you care about seriously.

The most well-informed decisions come from using all four of these steps. Different types, however, are inclined to emphasize some steps, and skim over or ignore others.

The priorities of functions chart on page 18 will tell you which steps are likely to be the easiest for you (the steps that use your dominant and auxiliary), and which are likely to be the most difficult for you (the steps that use your tertiary and least-preferred functions). The two middle letters of your type formula typically point to the steps that are easier. An INFP, for example, would likely find the Feeling and Intuition steps to be easier, but the Sensing and Thinking steps, representing the INFP's less-preferred functions, would make those steps more difficult or less interesting.

Definitely pay attention to the steps that are most natural and comfortable for you. It is *also* important to pay attention to the steps you are most likely to skip. Are you the ESFJ who may miss the new and different possibilities and to forget to take a tough-minded look at the consequences of some of your decisions? Or are you the ENTP who may miss attending to the facts of the situation and to forget to listen to what you truly care about?

Naturally, you will find yourself working through the steps more than once. For example, doing a tough-minded Thinking analysis of one of your options may let you know that you need to go back to gather more concrete Sensing information about that option.

Using the Zig-Zag process will give you a better understanding of the road you are following so that the next steps toward finding and managing your career will be clearer.

Setting Goals and Taking Action

Once you have made some career decisions you need to move to the planning and action steps. These next steps usually involve three things: (1) setting your career goals, (2) breaking those goals down into smaller goals and tasks, and then (3) taking concrete action on those subgoals.

Step One: *Set your career goals*

In this step you clarify where you are going. Long-term career goals you set in this step might be broad or specific, for example:

- mechanical engineer working for an airline

- police detective in a large city

- salesperson for an import auto dealer

- carpenter working for a small company that does residential work

- move from customer service to a training position in my company

- build my own business doing Web design

At this point what are your long-term career goals? What career(s) or career options do you want to pursue, or would you rather make changes within your current career?

YOUR CAREER GOALS. *What career(s) or career options do you want to pursue, or would you rather make changes within your current career?*

_____
_____
_____
_____
_____
_____
_____
_____
_____
_____
_____
_____
_____
_____

Step Two: *Break your goals down into smaller goals and tasks*

In this step, you determine what subgoals you need to complete and things you need to do in order for you to reach your longer-term goals. For example, some of the subgoals and tasks for the person pursuing a career in engineering could include:

- learn more about the specialty of mechanical engineering
- find out what courses are required to get into an engineering program
- gather information on specific companies
- write a résumé and cover letters and set up interviews

At this point what are your subgoals? That is, what are other short-term goals you have to reach and tasks you have to carry out before you can reach your long-term goals? Use the space below to write about your subgoals.

Step Three: *Take action*

In this third step, you get energized to take concrete action to reach your subgoals In general, taking action would involve actually making those telephone calls, going on information interviews, filling out job applications, writing résumés, getting training, marketing yourself, meeting with an employer to discuss changing your current job, or taking the steps needed to create your own job.

Get going! Remember, there is a time to reflect (Introversion) and a time to act (Extraversion). Make a commitment and begin acting on your subgoals *now*.

On the following pages are a list of strengths and blind spots that may be associated with your type preferences as you go through these planning and action steps.

YOUR SUBGOALS. *What are other short-term goals you have to reach and tasks you have to carry out before you can reach your long-term goals?*

EXTRAVERSION (E)

Strengths

- May move readily to the action phases
- Just pick up the phone and call people
- Present in interviews as energetic and self-confident
- Respond well to spontaneous aspects of interviews
- Learn well by trial and error

Blind Spots

- May act too quickly without reflecting
- May talk too much and not listen enough in interviews
- May become enticed by the external world—what's available—and lose sight of plans made based on self-reflection
- May talk too much and not listen enough in interviews—may overwhelm interviewers
- May not appear thoughtful enough in interviews

INTROVERSION (I)

Strengths

- May be naturally planful and willing to reflect on steps needed
- May look thoughtful and concerned with precision as they answer interview questions
- May present self well in writing
- May prepare well for interviews
- May communicate patience and appear calm

Blind Spots

- May stay too long in the planning stages and not spend enough time acting on ideas
- May not explore, take advantage of, or enjoy networking activities
- May isolate themselves and not seek input from others
- May not respond as well to parts of the interview that are unexpected
- May appear too reserved or serious in interviews

SENSING (S)

Strengths

- May make good use of concrete career goals and be thorough and efficient in follow-up
- May have a good understanding of the reality issues of the potential career or role (for example, educational requirements or job duties)
- May remember and make use of data and facts well, both in planning and in interview
- Respond well to specific interview questions about job experiences and job history

Blind Spots

- May get locked in to one perception of how career exploration/development is to be approached
- May focus too much on job history and past experience as they look at possible career roles
- May have difficulty with interview questions that ask for speculation outside area of expertise "what if" questions

INTUITION (N)

Strengths

- May become very enthusiastic about new and alternative career possibilities that show up during planning or interview
- May be very good at setting up long-term goals
- May be very convincing in verbally presenting your competencies during an interview, even when speculating outside your area of expertise (especially Extraverts)

Blind Spots

- May see too many possibilities or take too long to see "you can't get there from here"
- May underestimate or leave out important pragmatic steps in setting and achieving goals
- May have difficulty answering interview questions asking for specifics of job training and job history

THINKING (T)

Strengths

- May be willing to weigh all the options—even the unpleasant ones—when doing research on a career or employer
- Communicate competencies well on paper or in person
- May be good at standing one's ground in a tough interview
- Appear very task oriented and analytical in interview

Blind Spots

- May ignore useful information if the interviewer does not meet one's expectations of competence
- May appear too task oriented in the interview and not sensitive to interpersonal concerns involved in the position
- May neglect attending to the impact the job may have on relationships or personal values

FEELING (F)

Strengths

- May be willing and able to make use of networks and relationships
- May present in interview as warm, sensitive, and personal
- May read the expectations and needs of the interviewer
- Communicate enthusiasm and willingness to be personally involved in the goals of the organization

Blind Spots

- May expect personal contacts to win a job
- May take tough interviews personally
- May present in interview as too warm and not as someone who is task-oriented enough to get the job done

JUDGING (J)

Strengths

- May be good at planning tasks and subgoals for reaching larger goals
- May be good at meeting deadlines and achieving tasks
- May communicate a willingness to get things done and to take on responsibility during interviews

Blind Spots

- May be impatient with exploring options and move to premature closure
- May appear too structured or rigid in an interview
- May mistake efficiency for effectiveness in their planning, taking action, and in interviews

PERCEIVING (P)

Strengths

- May be able to respond to the need for changing plans and tasks as career search proceeds
- May be open to see and act on options that emerge during Interviews
- May have a spontaneous interviewing style and appear flexible and adaptable

Blind Spots

- May feel tied down by decisions and goals and be unwilling to make them
- May not appreciate that some career tasks may need to be completed by certain deadlines
- May seem not goal directed enough in interviews or may appear unfocused in career plans

Selling Your Differences

One of the basic lessons of psychological type is that people of different types have different and equally valuable talents. Further, those differences are advantageous and can be used in constructive ways. From this perspective, individual differences become selling points as you go about the action stages of your career search. The purpose of this section is to help you recognize and respect your strengths, and to encourage you to sell your differences.

Whether you are looking for your first job, modifying your role in your current organization, or changing careers later in life, you will need to sell yourself. That is, you will need to be able to assess your own personality and skills, and communicate your strengths clearly to others. Selling yourself means building on the natural strengths of who you are.

How do you identify and sell your differences? One way is to build on what you now know about type. You can look back at the descriptions given for the preferences, look at the individual type descriptions, and use type language to identify and communicate your strengths. This information is useful in filling out applications, in writing résumés or cover letters, and in interviewing.

For example, an ISTJ might say:

"I become very dedicated to my work and I am very task oriented."

"I like responsibility and I am thorough in my work."

"I have a great respect for the facts, and I attend to the bottom line to determine if a job is done."

In contrast, an ESFP might sell different strengths with the following statements:

"I have excellent people skills."

"I take a realistic and pragmatic approach to solving problems, and I am very good at trouble-shooting."

"I am a team player, and can be very good at managing conflict at work."

As you can see in the examples above, each person is communicating about a different set of skills, yet each is communicating that they are indeed a skilled and worthwhile person with whom to work. Remember, you bring your own natural set of gifts to a career. Some of these are gifts of your type, while others are talents, skills, and qualities that are not about type—but are a part of who you are and what you've experienced.

If you have worked through the sections of this booklet, then at this point you have been through some of the major steps of the career exploration and development process. You have looked at yourself through the dimensions of type, values, interests, skills, and type dynamics/development. You have seen some of the career patterns for your type, and you have gathered information on careers that interest you. You then saw how type plays into decision making and how type can affect your planning and taking action.

If you have worked through some (or all) of these steps, you are a lot further along than when you started. Congratulations! Now ask yourself if you are really through yet. It is important to stop and evaluate how this process has worked for you. Does it feel right and has it provided you with what you needed for now? You can always cycle back and gather more information on both yourself and prospective careers, and then you can make even more informed decisions, and take even more relevant action. You may also decide to seek the services of a career counselor to help you through some of the steps of your career exploration, decision making, planning, and taking action.

At the back of this book you will find a list of further resources for looking at yourself and careers from the perspective of psychological type. Best wishes in your career pursuits!

NOTES

NOTES

NOTES

NOTES

If you want to take the MBTI® assessment, the publisher, CPP, Inc., offers an online version where the type verification process is a part of the assessment. To learn more, go to www.mbticomplete.com

Center for Applications of Psychological Type (CAPT®) offers a program called "Take the MBTI Online" that provides:

- Online administration of the instrument
- Feedback materials which provide detailed introductory information regarding the MBTI instrument and psychological type:
  - Verifying Your Type Preferences (handout)
  - Descriptions of the Sixteen Types (handout)
  - *Looking at Type®: The Fundamentals* by Dr. Charles R. Martin (64 pg. paperback)
- A one-hour person-to-person feedback session, with a Certified MBTI® Practitioner
- A personalized interpretive report, detailing results and reported type

To learn more, go to http://www.capt.org/take-mbti-assessment/mbti.htm

The Murphy-Meisgeier Type Indicator for Children® (MMTIC®) assessment is designed to assess psychological type preferences for school age students through high school. Support materials include student workbooks and career reports for each of the 16 types. To learn more, go to www.capt.org

There are several publications written on the topic of psychological type that provide excellent information related to career exploration and selection for both students and teachers:

Discovering Type with Teens by Mollie Allen, Claire Hayman and Kay Abella. Gainesville, FL: Center for Applications of Psychological Type, 2009.

Gifts Differing by Isabel Briggs Myers with Peter B. Myers. Palo Alto, CA: Consulting Psychologists Press, Inc., 1995.

Great Minds Don't Think Alike! by Diane Payne and Sondra VanSant. Gainesville, FL: Center for Applications of Psychological Type, 2009.

Lifetypes by Sandra Hirsh and Jean Kummerow. New York: Warner Books, 1989.

Looking at Type®: The Fundamentals by Charles R. Martin. Gainesville, FL: Center for Applications of Psychological Type, 1997.

People Types & Tiger Stripes (4th edition) by Gordon D. Lawrence. Gainesville, FL: Center for Applications of Psychological Type, 2009.

Type for Life® Guide Navigating Your Career by Charles R. Martin. Gainesville, FL: Center for Applications of Psychological Type, 2010.

For further information on the Myers-Briggs Type Indicator® instrument or to purchase books and materials contact:

Center for Applications of Psychological Type, Inc.
2815 N.W. 13th Street, Suite 401
Gainesville, Florida 32609
www.capt.org
352.375.0160

ABOUT THE PUBLISHER

The Center for Applications of Psychological Type, Inc. (CAPT®) was established in the summer of 1975 with two major goals: to help make what is already known about psychological types useful in practical ways and to create new knowledge. Its founders, Isabel Briggs Myers and Mary H. McCaulley, adopted "the constructive use of differences" as the motto for this non-profit organization.

CAPT educates the public and professionals to view differences constructively by maintaining a number of services for use in education, counseling, organizational development, religious life, and research.

- CAPT houses the Isabel Briggs Myers Memorial Library, the largest collection of MBTI® publications, dissertations, and theses in the world. Research services are also available through the Library.

- CAPT publishes and distributes papers and books related to research and practical applications of the Indicator. Ongoing research is conducted and made available through new products and services.

- CAPT training offers basic and advanced training workshops and courses for managers, educators, counselors, psychotherapists, career counselors, psychologists, organizational development consultants, and religious leaders.

For more information about CAPT, visit our Web site at **www.capt.org.**

You can also order a print catalog by calling **800.777.2278.**

ABOUT THE AUTHOR

Charles Martin, Ph.D., is a licensed psychologist who uses type as a tool to help clients improve the quality of their lives and to help individuals and organizations enhance their performance. He is a consultant and trainer for the Center for Applications of Psychological Type and conducts MBTI® Certification Programs and other MBTI training workshops nationally and internationally. He is also the author and co-author of several popular books on the applications of type, including, *Looking at Type®: The Fundamentals, Building People, Building Programs*, and *Out of the Box: Exercises for Mastering the Power of Type to Build Effective Teams.*

CAPT®

Center for Applications of Psychological Type, Inc. ¦ 2815 N.W. 13th St., Suite 401 ¦ Gainesville, FL 32609
352.375.0160 ¦ 800.777.2278 *(toll-free USA and Canada only)* ¦ 352.378.0503 *(fax)* ¦ www.capt.org

Simple, Memorable, Applicable . . .

*The Looking at Type® books clearly explain the concepts
of psychological type and how to apply them in everyday life.*

Looking at Type®: The Fundamentals
Charles R. Martin

Looking at Type®: The Fundamentals provides a clear and easy
to understand overview of psychological type as measured by
the well-known Myers-Briggs Type Indicator® and Murphy-
Meisgeier Type Indicator for Children® assessments. Insights
gained from this book can enrich relationships, aid the decision-
making process, and increase a sense of self-worth and personal
competence. The book includes the basic nature of type as a
dynamic model of personality and lifelong development. Each
of the 16 type descriptions indicates unique paths to personal
growth, achievement, and applications for daily living.

Looking at Type®
Earle C. Page

When you understand the differences between the preferences
that make up the 16 psychological types, what initially appears
complex quickly becomes quite clear. This ever popular book
sticks to the basics and only describes the eight preferences
by using simple—yet precise—words to draw important
distinctions. The friendly graphics communicate the essence
of the preferences at a glance. This book is perfect for anyone
who has taken the MBTI® instrument and needs a friendly, easy-
to-access way for understanding their results.

Looking at Type® and Learning Styles
Gordon D. Lawrence

Written for both students and teachers, this book helps reveal personal learning styles in order to develop more effective study and test-taking strategies, and help teachers facilitate learning. Includes discussions on strengths, key motivators, and blind spots for different preferences and provides guidelines to assist teachers in curriculum development and delivery. Think of this as your guide to doing your best learning—or teaching!

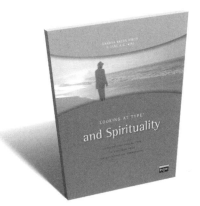

Looking at Type® and Spirituality
Sandra Krebs Hirsh and Jane A. G. Kise

Are you excited by active expression of your spirituality, or are you more interested in opportunities for reflection upon the divine? Learn more about how psychological type preferences can have a powerful impact on how you express your spirituality, common stumbling blocks to spirituality, and how your spirituality can grow deeper.

Looking at Type® in the Workplace
Larry Demarest

A fundamental introduction to how an individual's psychological type affects daily interactions at work and can influence everyday workplace activities such as responding to conflict, work style, being part of a team, making decisions, dealing with change, and communication.

Looking at Type® Series
You can get the entire series in one package, which includes one each of *Looking at Type®: The Fundamentals, Looking at Type®: Your Career, Looking at Type® and Learning Styles, Looking at Type® and Spirituality, and Looking at Type® in the Workplace.*

For more information
call CAPT at 800.777.2278 or 352.375.0160, or visit www.capt.org

typefor**Life**®

Now that you know your type, what's next?

What do those four letters mean, and how can you apply them to your daily life? Those letters are just the beginning! Each of CAPT's new *Type for Life® Guides* provides a highly readable way of understanding how your personality type shapes your approach to life.

Each guide focuses on a particular aspect of life, and each guide is specific to your four-letter personality type:

- **Discovering You**: How your personality shapes your approach to life

- **Navigating Your Career**: How understanding your personality leads to a more rewarding work life

- **Resolving Conflict**: How your personality influences difficult interactions with other people

- **Building Better Relationships**: Using the lens of personality to help couples thrive—a guide for two

Personality type gives you a portrait of your own uniqueness. *Type for Life® Guides* help you navigate life using personality type as your guide.

Ready to begin the journey? *Type for Life® Guides* are available exclusively through the CAPT website: **www.capt.org**

Learn more about using type in everyday life at the new CAPT *Type for Life®* blog: **www.capt.org/type-for-life-blog/**

Center for Applications of Psychological Type, Inc. • 800.777.2278 • www.capt.org